W9-BIH-512

THE LITTLE BOOK

OF
STOCK MARKET
CYCLES

Little Book Big Profits Series

In the *Little Book Big Profits* series, the brightest icons in the financial world write on topics that range from tried-and-true investment strategies to tomorrow's new trends. Each book offers a unique perspective on investing, allowing the reader to pick and choose from the very best in investment advice today.

Books in the *Little Book Big Profits* series include:

THE LITTLE BOOK

OF
STOCK MARKET
CYCLES

How to Take Advantage of
Time-Proven Market Patterns

JEFFREY A. HIRSCH

WILEY
John Wiley & Sons, Inc.

Published by John Wiley & Sons, Inc., Hoboken, New Jersey.
Published simultaneously in Canada.

For general information on our other products and services or for technical support, please contact our
Customer Care Department within the United States at (800) 762-2974, outside the United States at
(317) 572-3993 or fax (317) 572-4002.

Wiley also publishes its books in a variety of electronic formats. Some content that appears in print
may not be available in electronic books. For more information about Wiley products, visit our web site
at www.wiley.com.

ISBN 978-1-118-27011-0 (cloth); 978-1-18-28349-3 (ebk);
978-1-118-28485-8 (ebk); 978-1-118-28624-1 (ebk)

Printed in the United States of America

10 9 8 7 6 5 4 3 2 1

For Jennifer and our two boys,
Samson and Nathaniel

Contents

Foreword

⟨~⟩

IT MIGHT SEEM ODD that a fundamentally oriented investor would write the Foreword for a book devoted to technical analysis. After all, many fundamental investors view technical analysis as nothing more than fortune-telling, and technical analysts as wizards who should be locked up and kept away from the children (and investors/traders who behave like children). But here I am, a fundamental investor, doing just that.

The fact is that the business of investing is complicated. Think of it as a pyramid with each angle of the pyramid representing a different approach—you've got the fundamentals, valuation, and the technicals.

It is the influence on equities called the "technicals" that Jeff Hirsch captures so eloquently and succinctly in *The Little Book of Stock Market Cycles.*

Jeff's thoughtful book takes a cue from Winston Churchill, who once wrote that "the farther back you can look, the farther forward you are likely to see."

As Jeff writes, the lessons of stock market history are invaluable. The study of patterns from the past makes future trends clearer, just as the avoidance of history makes them potentially lethal to your investments' well-being.

Mr. Market is not an easy guy to get to know. Analysis of market history and the rhythm of financial cycles isn't a simple task, and especially not the way Jeff does it. Determining the roles that human behavior, holidays, elections, seasons, and the calendar play in influencing the stock market's direction requires careful observation and critical thinking. Even the role of peace and war is fair game in Jeff's analysis.

And then there is Jeff's outlandish May 2010 prophesy of a super boom in stocks—in which he feels the Dow Jones Industrial Average may rise to 38,820 by 2025!

Learn why Jeff is ringing in a new bull market beginning in the 2017–2018 period. His conviction is high and his reasoning appears sound.

In *The Little Book of Stock Market Cycles,* Jeff presents a commonsense message and invaluable lessons for how to take advantage of time-proven market patterns. Both individual and institutional investors should take notice.

After all, those who cannot remember the past are condemned to repeat it!

Douglas A. Kass
Seabreeze Partners Management Inc.

Introduction

THERE IS NO MAGIC formula to make trading or investing easy. Nothing can replace research, experience, and a healthy dose of luck. There is, however, a methodology investors can employ to mitigate losses and enhance returns. Nineteenth century philosopher George Santayana once pronounced that "Those who cannot remember the past are condemned to repeat it."

This is the cornerstone of my research for the *Stock Trader's Almanac*, which was founded by my father Yale Hirsch in 1966. By analyzing and studying the markets from a historical perspective, modern-day market action and events can be put into historical context. Whether you are a short-term trader or a longer term investor, being aware of historical and seasonal patterns and tendencies is helpful and valuable.

The Little Book of Stock Market Cycles is an amalgamation of the most effective indicators, patterns, and seasonalities that have been painstakingly researched and vetted over the nearly 50-year history of the *Stock Trader's Almanac*. Those who study market history are bound to profit from it!

To be a successful trader or investor, you must understand how the market behaves under normal conditions. Whether it is in a secular bull market or a secular bear market, Wall Street moves to a predictable cadence governed by the passage of time. Recurring events such as the presidential election every four years, end-of-quarter portfolio rebalancing, options and futures expirations, tax deadlines, and holidays have a predictable influence on traders and investors.

People's day-to-day lives, such as paying bills, going on summer vacations, holiday shopping, and 401(k) contributions have an indelible effect on the market. Humans are creatures of habit. Knowing the habits of your fellow traders and investors will make market events, once dismissed as chance, unfold before you with apparent outcomes. Even in today's world of "high frequency" trading and 4G smart phone communication, old-time daily regimens prevail and shape the intraday moments of the stock market in much the same manner as they have for decades.

Exogenous events, whether foreign or domestic, have been impacting the market since our forefathers gathered under the buttonwood tree. In today's geopolitical cauldron, an investor who doesn't comprehend the difference between peacetime markets and wartime markets is a sitting duck. Though the market never reacts the same way every time, knowing how it performed in the past will give you an edge in future times of crisis.

However, this is not an exact science as patterns and tendencies change and shift. Major cultural shifts and technology have had a profound impact on markets and their behaviors. Farming made August the best month of the year from 1900 to 1951, but now that less than 2 percent of the U.S. population farms, August is one of the worst months. Technology has increased access to markets and significantly speeded its response. In 1965, millions of shares were traded daily on the NYSE, now it is billions.

Armed with the knowledge of how the market has performed in the past, you will be better prepared to identify shifts in momentum that come at major market tops and bottoms. Your long-term investments will grow quicker and safer while your trading activities will become more productive and profitable. This *Little Book* will show you the market's behavior and how to incorporate it into your investment strategy.

As Patrick Henry said in his famous "Give Me Liberty or Give Me Death" speech, "I know of no way of judging the future but by the past." Market cycles and patterns do not repeat exactly what they have done in the past, but like the rest of the natural phenomena in the universe, they surely rhyme.

Within these pages I have given you the framework of what makes the market tick and how it behaves with respect to human and cultural behavior patterns. I don't blindly subscribe to dogmatic schools of market cycles with rigid counting systems. Like my good friend Sam Stovall at S&P, I use history as a guide.

Always remember that stock market cycles are not exact, they are as much an art form as a science. Be contrary to the crowd. When everyone is in agreement and dead sure a particular cycle, level, or future outcome is in play, the market will likely wobble off course and do what the least number of market participants expect.

Once you have these cycles and patterns firmly embedded in your investment and trading mentality you must turn to the factors on the ground in the present. Using common sense, technical indicators, fundamentals, and contrary thinking you will be able anticipate the future with success.

Trade carefully, invest wisely, and use history as a guide!

Chapter One

Cutting through the Bull

~

Exploring the Meaning and History behind Bull and Bear Markets

HAVE YOU EVER HEARD the saying "a rising tide lifts all boats"? When referring to economics and the financial markets, it means that everyone does better in prosperous times and most stocks perform well in bull markets. Conversely, all boats drop when the tide goes out. Most folks feel the pain of economic recession and bear markets drive stocks down en masse.

"Financial genius is a rising stock market" is another saying I keep in mind to help contain any bouts of hubris that arise from making accurate market calls. The phrase has been attributed to both the renowned economist John Kenneth Galbraith and the legendary investor Sir John Templeton. Put another way, "don't confuse brains with a bull market."

Being in a bull or a bear market has the single greatest influence on stock prices and the value of your investment portfolio. Therefore, it's critical for investors to know how to identify the two. What happened to your portfolio in 2008? Unless you were a superstar stock-shorting hedge fund manager your portfolio was likely cut in half like those of most investors and even top fund managers. If you panicked early and fast in 2008 like I did you minimized losses and rode out the storm in bonds and cash.

In addition to determining whether you are in a bull market or a bear market, it is equally as important to know what type of bull or bear market it is. Commentators use a lot of different terms to describe the markets and it's important to know what they are. We are currently in a secular bear market and have been since the year 2000. But what does that mean?

Describing the Markets

Is this the dawn of a new long-term secular bull market? Or is it merely a short-term cyclical bull in the midst of the overarching secular bear market we have been in since 2000? Answering this important question can give us a better understanding of how the market is likely to perform over the near term and the next several years. And if you're not familiar with the terms used to describe the markets, it's time to get up to speed.

Let's start with a couple of important definitions: secular and cyclical. According to the *Oxford English Dictionary*, "secular" means "of a fluctuation or trend: occurring or persisting over an unlimited period; not periodic or short-term," and "cyclical" means "belonging to a definite chronological cycle."

When it comes to the definition of secular and cyclical with respect to the markets, things become cloudy. That's because financial markets are malleable. Remember that these markets are run by imperfect human beings. Even though much trading is computer generated now, those computers and the software they run were designed and created by emotional creatures with needs, wants, desires, impatience, envy, vengeance, love, hate . . . you get the idea.

Therefore, secular and cyclical stock market patterns fluctuate and adhere to looser rules than many other disciplines. There is much debate over the definitions of bull and bear markets. But put simply, secular markets last a long time, usually 10 years or more. Cyclical markets last less than 10 years, usually less than 5. The longest cyclical market of the twentieth century lasted nearly eight years from October 1990 to July 1998. It was contained in the 1982 to 2000 secular bull market.

The distinguished team at Ned Davis Research (NDR) classifies a bull market as a 30 percent rise in the Dow Jones Industrial Average after 50 calendar days or a 13 percent rise after 155 calendar days. Similarly a bear market requires a 30 percent drop in the Dow Jones Industrial Average after 50 calendar days or 13 percent decline after 145 calendar days. Reversals of 30 percent in the Value Line Geometric Index since 1965 also qualify.

Standard & Poor's deems a move of plus or minus 20 percent for the equity bull and bear cycles. While the 20 percent equity move is the major criteria, there are other secondary issues (length of time, S&P 500 versus long-term moving averages, etc.) that are also considered.

However, defining secular bull and bear markets requires outside-the-box thinking. By my reckoning, secular markets span a period of about 8 to 20 years. I classify secular bulls as an extended period of years, when the stock market produces successive new highs and higher lows. Secular bears are often impacted by protracted military campaigns and financial crises, and the market is unable to reach a significant new high. (In Chapter Two, we'll discuss how war and peace impact the market). You can also ascertain the nature of the secular market, bull or bear, by analyzing the cyclical bull and bear markets within it.

Talking in Seculars

In Figure 1.1 the market is divided into eight secular periods since 1896, which is the year the Dow began. Secular bear trends are highlighted with shaded boxes.

Figure 1.1   Secular Market Trends Since 1896

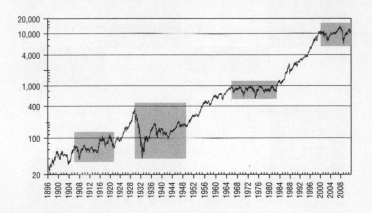

Four secular bull markets ran from 1896 to 1906, 1921 to 1929, 1949 to 1966, and 1982 to 2000. The four bears span 1906 to 1921, 1929 to 1949, 1966 to 1982, and 2000 to the present. We then lined up all the cyclical bulls and bears within the secular bull markets and compared them to those in secular bear markets.

Since 1896, cyclical bulls have averaged Dow gains of 105.4 percent during secular bull markets. Cyclical bulls

Figure 1.2   Dow Jones Industrials Secular Market Averages Since 1896

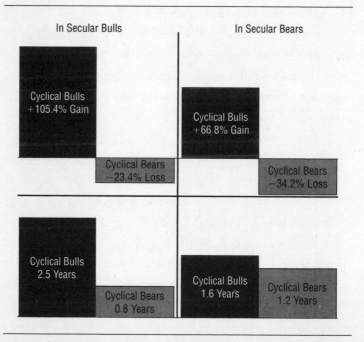

In Secular Bulls

In Secular Bears

Cyclical Bulls
+105.4% Gain

Cyclical Bulls
+66.8% Gain

Cyclical Bears
−23.4% Loss

Cyclical Bears
−34.2% Loss

Cyclical Bulls
2.5 Years

Cyclical Bears
0.8 Years

Cyclical Bulls
1.6 Years

Cyclical Bears
1.2 Years

were 60 percent greater, and nearly twice as long on average, as in secular bears. Cyclical bears on average were 50 percent worse and about two times longer in secular bears. (See Figure 1.2.)

For perspective, cyclical bulls have been weaker in secular bears since World War II. World War II created a tectonic shift in the economy and marketplace. Before the war the United States was predominantly a farming economy, but afterward it was a military-industrial complex, a technology powerhouse. What the United States becomes next remains to be seen.

In general, secular bulls are marked by short and timid cyclical bears and long, powerful cyclical bulls. Conversely, secular bears exhibit weak, fleeting cyclical bulls and protracted cyclical bears teeming with sharp, nasty sell-offs; failed rebounds; capitulation; brutish trading at bottoms; and often a lack of interest in stocks by the public.

We deem the current market since the top in 2000 a secular bear market. Since the year 2000, the Dow has had four cyclical bear markets of 29.7 percent, 31.5 percent, 53.8 percent, and 16.8 percent and three cyclical bulls of 29.1 percent, 94.4 percent, and 95.7 percent through 2011, recording the longest cyclical bull in a secular bear and worst cyclical bear since 1929 to 1932. The 95.7 percent bull move from March 2009 to April 2011 was hefty and was of average length of all cyclical bulls at just over two years long. This is reminiscent of the cyclical bulls during the secular bear from 1929 to 1949 and from 1934 to 1937 and from 1942 to 1946 during World War II. I don't believe we are in for such a protracted bear as the Great Depression, but I'm not yet convinced we've started a new secular bull trend, either.

Let's Shoot Some Bull

Now that we know the history of bull and bear markets since the Dow began, what we really want to know is when we can expect the next big secular bull that will get us out of the post-financial-crisis funk. The new secular bull will not emerge and lasting prosperity will not take charge until there is an extended period of relative peace.

Part of the problem is that the United States is still entangled in a protracted foreign military campaign in Afghanistan. The good news is that our presence in Afghanistan is winding down. And with Bin Laden gone and the "Arab Spring" blossoming, the broader war on terror is at bay. We can't be naïve and think that our problems in that region of the world and other hotspots are over, but at least massive military combat troop deployment is down and no longer monopolizes our headlines.

This has been the consistent theme in all of the previous secular bear periods: 1906 to 1921 (World War I), 1929 to 1949 (World War II), and 1966 to 1982 (Vietnam).

War is not necessarily the initial event that starts the secular bear period, but the market has not begun a new secular bull period until the war is over and the postwar inflation kicks in.

Finally, all of these previous secular bull trends were accompanied by a major paradigm shift from an enabling technology or cultural change. By 1896 the rails had connected the coasts and commerce, trade, and people flowed like never before. In the Roaring Twenties the motion picture industry inspired the planet with the advent of "talkies," while Lindbergh and Earhart mesmerized the world with trans-Atlantic air travel and automobiles unshackled the middle class.

In the post-World War II bull period, consumerism took hold, the population exploded with the baby boom, and America helped rebuild Europe and Japan. Space projects and countless industrial technology innovations spurred growth and TV connected people around the world. The age of information powered the super bull of the 1980s and 1990s. Personal computers, telecommunications, and the Internet empowered and liberated individuals and society. Only the future will tell what will fuel the next boom.

Seeing What Tomorrow Brings

Where does that leave us today? Since there does not appear to be a new enabling technology or cultural shift on the horizon and the U.S. military is still deeply involved overseas, it's not yet clear.

Perhaps when we finally exit Iraq and Afghanistan, provided we have not just moved our armed forces over to Iran or somewhere else, and a new game-changing innovation or way of life ignites the planet, then we will begin a new secular bull trend. For now, we will most likely remain trapped in the current trading range and are poised for a cyclical bear market or two in this secular bear trend that could bring us down 20 to 30 percent over the next five or six years.

At a Glance

- Being in a bull or bear market is the single greatest influence on stock prices.
- Secular market trends are long-term, usually lasting 8 to 20 years. Cyclical market trends are shorter-term, lasting anywhere from a few months to several years.
- During secular bull markets, cyclical bear markets are mostly short and shallow. Cyclical bull markets are long and strong.
- During secular bear markets, cyclical bulls are usually brief and mild. Cyclical bear markets are dragged out and deep.

Chapter Two

War and Peace

*How War and Peace (and Inflation)
Impact the Market*

WITHOUT A DOUBT, THE single most important enduring influence on the stock market is war. For as long as the United States has been embroiled in a significant and lasting military combat operation, the stock market has failed to make any significant headway. And so it bodes well for the markets that more than a decade of foreign conflict following the September 2001 terrorist attacks is drawing to an end.

But this is not just true for today's markets. The impact of war and peace and inflation has been the driving force in creating the cycle of booms and busts for the past two centuries and beyond. What makes the market range-bound during wartime and causes it to rise during peacetime? The answer is inflation. The government empties the treasury during a war. It also focuses on foreign or war-related issues rather than domestic concerns and the economy. The result is a sustained rise in inflation. Only after the economy settles down and the country refocuses on domestic issues does the stock market soar to new heights.

Creatures of Habit

Human history is replete with episodes of economic booms and busts and the rise and fall of societies. For millennia, starting well before the Common Era, complex civilizations produced massive structures, innovative technology, and cultural feats of education, literature, math, science, and philosophy only to suffer their own demise. Rome fell, the Dark Ages shrouded Europe for five centuries, the Hans were replaced, the Maya disappeared, and the Soviet Union collapsed. Tremendous advancements in technology have not shielded modern civilization from volatility. War and financial panics have been an even greater force in the shaping of humanity during the twentieth century, and thus far, the twenty-first century.

Ancient ingenuity and customs are embedded in the flourishing cultures and societies that now exist, revered by the people who inhabit the places their ancestors once dwelled. The pharaohs are long gone, but the Pyramids of Giza are still a sought-after site for tourists and archeologists alike. Mexicans still celebrate the Aztec creation myth of Quetzalcoatl, the feathered-serpent deity. Thirty miles northeast of Mexico City in Teotihuacan, California hippies practice sun salutations on the Pyramid of the Sun, the third-largest pyramid in the world built in the first century.

Classical Greek culture permeates Western civilization. Colonial European empirical influence endures throughout the world it flattened. Yoga practiced in strip malls and fitness centers across the United States has its roots in traditional disciplines that originated 4,000 to 5,000 years ago in the Indus River Valley Civilization that now encompasses Pakistan, India, Afghanistan, and Iran. Throughout all this amazing history, the human condition has been explosive at times and stable at other times.

The Dark Ages were followed by a long period of medieval conquest, barbarian invasions, crusades, and religious zealotry before yielding to the Renaissance, the Age of Enlightenment, two industrial revolutions, railroad booms, and the Gilded Age. Exponential economic expansion and growth of the eighteenth and nineteenth centuries was plagued by a host of wars, panics, and depressions.

The American Revolution and the birth of this great nation created massive inflation followed by a nine-year period of prosperity and world peace from 1783 to 1792. Then international conflict and civil strife cast a pall over the world. Incredible far-reaching technological achievements contributed to the creation of massive wealth for industrialists, business magnates, and tycoons. But war and financial panics truncated the evolution of the middle class. Massive inflation brought on by the American Civil War contributed to the Reconstruction era boom from 1863 to 1873 as the transcontinental railroad, completed in 1869, connected America from coast to coast.

The financial Panic of 1873 kicked off a worldwide economic depression that lasted into 1896, known in the United States as the Long Depression. The National Bureau of Economic Research lists the contraction from October 1873 to March 1879 at 65 months, the longest in their records, eclipsing the 43-month contraction of the Great Depression. Much like during the Panic of 1873, rampant speculation, railroad overbuilding, and dubious financing practices ushered in another depression in 1893 that caused double-digit unemployment for the next five to six years.

As the nineteenth century wound to a close, the advent of telegraph, railroads, telephone, internal combustion engines, automobiles, ocean liners, electric light bulbs, and radio laid the groundwork for what some called "The Greatest Century That Ever Was." War and peace, manias and slumps, inflation and innovation have always impacted economics, wealth, and the markets. But when the new Dow Jones Industrial Average was published for the first time on May 26, 1896, we had for the first time a consistent, trackable index that could objectively measure in real time and over the long term the fluctuations of prosperity, the level of economic soundness, and the prospects for growth.

Still the most quintessential financial market gauge ever devised, this Dow Jones Industrial Average benchmark continued to mature over the next several decades in conjunction with the creation of the Federal Reserve System in 1913 and the advent of central banking. As the famous American humorist Will Rogers once quipped, "There have been three great inventions since the beginning of time: fire, the wheel, and central banking."

History never repeats itself exactly, but an understanding of stock market behavior during the three major wars of the twentieth century provides important insight into market action during the current war winding down in Iraq and Afghanistan, the broader war on terror, and the Arab Spring—the revolutionary wave of civil uprisings sweeping across the Arab world that began in December 2010 in Tunisia and continues today, most prominently in Syria.

War: What Is It Good For?

The Dow has never achieved a lasting high during wartime. The lack of a big breakout can be attributed to muted investor enthusiasm. Every time the market tried to break out of its range, inevitably a negative exogenous event pertaining to the war or other crisis dampened spirits (if the business cycle, economic weakness, or politics had not already done so). It has fleetingly poked above the previous highs as it did in 1973 and 2007, but the moves were short-lived and not sustained.

The war machine props up the market. After the initial shock of once again being in a war, the market forms a floor near the prewar low, or the reaction low, at the outset of the conflict. The combination of government spending, investor bargain hunting, and good old American pride have helped insulate the market from significantly breaching that early low. When World War I broke out on July 30, 1914, the Dow dropped 6.9 percent on the day to 52.32 (back adjusted to reflect Dow Jones Industrial Average change from 12 to 20 stocks in September 1916). That low was never seen again until well after World War I at the depths of the Great Depression in 1932 and 1933.

The March 31, 1938, pre-World War II low of 98.95 was only marginally surpassed by less than 1 percent on April 28, 1942—four months and three weeks after the Japanese bombed Pearl Harbor. On this day the Office of Price Administration froze prices on most goods and services in the United States, and President Franklin Roosevelt delivered the 21st of the 30 "fireside chats" he gave from just after his inauguration in March 1933 to just after D-Day in June 1944. Entitled "On Sacrifice," this chat focused on losses in the Pacific and uncertainty in Europe. He called on Americans to maintain their resolve during the war and warned that they would all have to sacrifice to meet the country's war needs.

President Kennedy's crackdown on steel price increases rocked Wall Street and knocked the Dow down 27 percent to 535.76 in June 1962. This low would hold throughout the Cuban Missile Crisis later that year, the Vietnam War, the stagflation of the 1970s and the double-dip recession of the early 1980s.

Markets rally on sustained good news and they fall on sustained bad news. The markets also tend to be more reactive early in wartime. By the end of a prolonged engagement, investors tend to be more callous to news. The markets also anticipate the end of the war by moving to a high-water mark. This contributes to the inevitable letdown when peace breaks out and the usual sell-off.

Wartime presidents do not lose. Presidents tend to shape their political decisions pertaining to a foreign war around the presidential election cycle making unpopular decisions only after they are reelected while creating as much good news as possible leading up to the election. The rhetoric from the incumbent administration is always that conditions are improving, while challengers call for change. Domestic issues, a weak ticket from the incumbent party, low approval ratings for the president, and the lack of a sitting president or strong VP running, ushered a new party into the White House in 2008. Like Harding in 1920, FDR in 1932, and Nixon in 1968, Obama came into office with a country clamoring for change. It remains to be seen, but that may also be the case in 2012.

The markets have been stuck in a trading range since the dotcom stock market bubble popped in 2000 and the Iraq War began on March 19, 2003. While there have been large rallies and pullbacks, there has been no real advance since 2000, and the April 1997 low of Dow 6391.69 has not been breached. Moves that leave the previous highs behind for good—the greater than 500 percent moves that have historically occurred between all of the major wars the United States has been involved in—have not happened.

Figure 2.1 500+ Percent Moves Follow Inflation

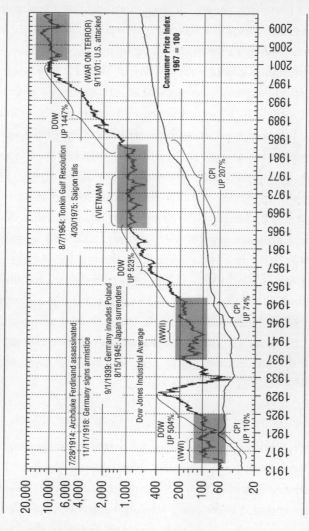

Source: © *Stock Trader's Almanac*. CPI source: Bureau of Labor Statistics.

Figure 2.1 shows the big picture. The Dow and the Consumer Price Index are plotted together with high-lighted sections showing the long-term range-bound markets surrounding World War I, World War II, and Vietnam. The long super booms and bull markets are bracketed with the Dow's performance. The correlation between war, inflation, and the subsequent catch-up of the market is impossible to ignore. Consolidations surrounding war-times possess roughly the same percentage range. These give the appearance of launching pads for the 500 percent moves. The inflation/catch-up correlation is clear. World War I inflation (up 110 percent) was followed by the 504 percent rise in the stock prices during the 1920s. The inflation of World War II (up 74 percent) preceded the subsequent rise of the Dow of 523 percent. Finally, the inflation due to the Vietnam conflict (as well as oil embargoes and the infamous stagflation of the 1970s) of over 200 percent and the subsequent super bull is a hopeful reminder as well as a warning to all investors.

To Boldly Go Where the Dow Has Never Gone

I first realized that we were setting up for the next 500 percent move in September 2002 during the first major downdraft of this now 12-year-old secular bear market. Over the next eight years I wrote extensively on the long, sideways period in which the market was destined to remain. This culminated in my Super Boom forecast that was first released in May 2010.

Based on the war, peace, and inflation market cycle related earlier, my analysis projects that the Dow will stay trapped in the current range visible in Figure 2.1 until 2017 or 2018. By that time major U.S. combat operations should be wrapped up and a period of relative world peace will be emerging. Inflation should have picked up and be leveling off. And some, yet-to-be-developed technology will be on the brink of transforming the planet like the car, TV, and microprocessor before it.

While we may not recognize it at first, the next economic boom will be under way, and the market will commence the bulk of the 500 percent move that will bring the Dow to 38,820 by the year 2025. From the 1974 bottom it took eight years for the boom to start and then another eight for the Dow to move up 500 percent. A 500 percent rise from the intraday low of 6,470 on March 6, 2009, would put the Dow at 38,820 in 2025. This number may sound ridiculous, but from the 2011 close of 12,218 it is only 8.6 percent each year, well within the historic average annual gain for the market.

At a Glance

- War, peace, and inflation have an indelible impact on the stock market. They are the foundation of the cycle of boom and bust and of secular bull and bear markets.
- During war, the market is trapped in a range unable to sustain a new high. When the war is over and inflation levels off the economy booms, fueled by peace and innovation. The market often soars 500 percent or more as it catches up with inflation.

Chapter Three

A Century of Booms and Busts

Examining Financial Panics and Economic Explosions of the Twentieth Century

BY TAKING A STROLL down memory lane and examining the history of the twentieth century we gain valuable perspective on how today's lingering economic malaise and turbulent geopolitical situation is most likely to resolve. It is well known that history repeats, though not exactly.

The state of affairs resembles different aspects of the three previous busts as well as some brand-new wrinkles.

The next boom phase will contain characteristics of earlier expansions and bull markets as well as some events we can't imagine. As we examine the past you may feel some déjà vu. This should provide some solace for the future as you realize stocks will rise to new lofty levels in the next decade. Once the hangover from the 2007 to 2009 financial crisis subsides, governments will begin to function effectively again, facilitating growth and innovation.

As the Century Turns

Financial markets began the twentieth century on a wild ride. Global volatility would moderate considerably during this century as the international playing field leveled off. But the early years were trying. A bear market from April 1899 to September 1900 that shaved 31.5 percent off the Dow heralded in the new century as immigrants fleeing oppression and turmoil in Europe flooded the United States at the rate of 100 per hour in 1900.

A brief nine-month bull market that lifted the Dow 48 percent ended in the Panic of 1901 as the battle to control the railroads caused a run on stocks and a market crash. Then, the Rich Man's Panic of 1903, a two-year recession, and two-and-a-half-year bear market drove the Dow down 46 percent to its low for the century. Bulls ruled the

Street for more than two years from November 1903 to January 1906 as the Dow gained 144 percent. Henry Ford founded Ford Motor in 1903, but production of his Model T would not occur until 1908 and the automobile would not liberate the world until after World War I. The internal combustion engine also powered the Wright Brother's flight at Kitty Hawk, North Carolina, in December 1903.

During this mini-boom real estate values soared in New York and antitrust battles were waged. Teddy Roosevelt began his antitrust suit against Standard Oil in 1906, which was finally broken up into 34 companies in 1911. The 1906 San Francisco earthquake also weighed on the economy. Then the Banker's Panic of 1907 slashed the Dow nearly in half, down 48.5 percent from January 1906 to November 1907. During this financial crisis the U.S. Treasury bought bonds to offset the decline and at the bottom J.P. Morgan orchestrated a cash infusion with other bankers to shore up stock prices; the Fed's maneuvers and government-engineered bailouts in 2008 were not much different.

The Dow rallied 90 percent over the next two years, but stalled just below the 1906 high as the secular bear market that would keep the Dow range-bound between 50 (adjusted for the new 1916 Dow) and 120 until 1925 took hold. Double-dip two-year recessions, from January 1910 to January 1912 and January 1913 to December 1914, squashed the economy and market as the federal government continued to reign in powerful corporate trusts. In 1913 Henry Ford's moving assembly line enabled mass production of automobiles and helped power the super boom of the Roaring Twenties. The onset of World War I closed the New York Stock Exchange for four months from the end of July to the beginning of December 1914, putting a floor under the market until the Great Depression.

World War I

After two years of war in the Balkans it was the assassination of Austrian Archduke Franz Ferdinand on June 28, 1914, that sparked World War I. A vast array of alliances and ambitions set off a domino effect as conflicts erupted across the world. The New York Stock Exchange closed from July 31, 1914, until December 12, 1914. Much of the escalation of the war occurred during this time. When the NYSE reopened, a bull market began as the United States maintained its neutrality in World War I and supported the Allied war effort over the next two years.

Germany's bombing of the United Kingdom on January 19, 1915, and sinking of a U.S. freighter on January 28 of the same year pushed the market down briefly. Stocks also took a dive when a German U-boat sank the British passenger ship *Lusitania*, killing 1,198 of the 1,959 on board, which turned international public opinion against Germany and began a process that would lead to U.S. entry into the war. Germany's bombing of Paris in January 1916 roiled the market for six months. But it was not until President Woodrow Wilson was elected to a second term in November 1916 and Germany made peace overtures in December 1916 that stocks ended the first bull market since the reopening of the market that had pushed the Dow up 110.5 percent to a new all-time high of 110.15 on November 21, 1916.

One of the 10 worst bear markets since 1900 ensued and knocked the Dow down 40 percent over the next 13 months as the war turned uglier. Germany began attacking neutral ships in the warzone and engaged in unrestricted submarine warfare in January 1917. Diplomatic relations with Germany were broken off in February and the United States declared war on April 6, 1917.

Conscription in the United States began in June 1917, and when President Wilson took control of nearly all the railroads the day after Christmas 1917, the low of the bear market was secured. The Dow rallied over 81 percent for nearly two years as Allied victories forced an end to the war. An armistice was signed Sunday, November 11, 1918, on what is now celebrated as Veterans Day. But the 1920s super boom would not commence until the final peace accord was signed between the United States and Germany in August 1921.

The Roaring Twenties

Driven by a 2,500 percent increase in government spending over three years, from when the U.S. entered World War I in 1917 until 1919, prices more than doubled with the Consumer Price Index up 110 percent from 1915 to 1920. Inflation settled down in the 1920s, but the economy and the stock market played catch-up. "Normalcy" was returned to politics as President Harding promised on the campaign trail and a dynamic nine years of artistic creativity, liberalization of social mores, and financial speculation carried the Dow up 504 percent from 1921 to 1929. Peacetime, inflation, political cooperation, and systemic changes in social and cultural behavior provided the base, but it was the sweeping array of enabling technology that ignited the boom.

Prohibition's ban on alcohol did little to quell its demand and usage. In fact, it created a taboo factor that fueled organized crime and speculative fervor. But it was the next amendment to the Constitution—the Nineteenth Amendment in 1920, giving women the right to vote— that had a much greater positive impact on the country. Women not only voted, this newfound equality inspired women to work more, providing many families with two incomes and more money to spend in the new age of consumerism.

Laissez-faire government growth policies allowed industry and business to thrive, but it was the new enabling technologies that became available to the middle class that powered the 1920s boom. It was the mass production of the automobile, making cars affordable for the middle class, that was the single most important cultural paradigm-shifting event. Movies and radio skyrocketed. The government funded new road and highway infrastructure projects to carry all the cars. Electric and telephone lines were strung across the nation. Power plants were constructed and cities of all sizes grew as new industries, business, and construction sprung up from coast to coast.

All this expansion and innovation created an air of invincibility that fanned the flames of rampant speculation and irresponsible financial activity. For six consecutive years from October 1923 to September 1929 the Dow marched steadily higher, despite two relatively mild recessions from 1923 to 1924 and 1927 to 1928. At the height of the final six-year bull market with the Dow up 344.5 percent—still more than the 294.8 percent in 1990 to 1998—individual investors could buy stocks on 90 percent margin.

It all came crashing down October 28 and 29, 1929, with a run on stocks that caused the worst crash in the history of the New York Stock Exchange. The Dow fell 23.0 percent in two days and 47.9 percent in 71 days. All booms come to an end, but never before or since in such dramatic fashion. This lesson of unbridled speculation and lax oversight of financial markets has yet to be fully learned.

And Then Depression Set In

At 71 days short, the Great Crash of 1929 would hold the record for the shortest bear market for 58 years until the Crash of October 1987 nearly matched the two-day affair in 1929 with a one-day 22.6 percent plunge. But Black Monday 1987 marked the end of the 55-day bear, culminating in a 36.1 percent Dow loss, and was a mere blip in the super boom of the 1980s and 1990s. The Crash of 1929 was just the first wave of the decline and a tepid five-month bull market ran out of steam in April 1930.

Ethical abuses and financial shenanigans surfaced on Wall Street and the crash gathered momentum again. Fallout from the loss of billions of dollars of wealth in one day after a decade of exponential expansion in the 1920s, the meteoric rise of the stock market, and unbridled speculation shattered investor confidence for years. The decline in stock prices was so swift and devastating that it disrupted commerce, causing bankruptcies, business closures, frozen credit, job losses, depressed consumer spending, bank failures, and severe deflation.

A major drought began consuming North American prairie lands from Canada to Texas in 1930, crushing agricultural prices. Coupled with poor farming practices this drought turned into the Dust Bowl that destroyed 100 million acres from 1930 to 1936 in and around the panhandles of Texas and Oklahoma. Stocks plunged like at no other time in modern history, suffering huge double-digit losses four years straight during President Hoover's entire term in office. No other presidential term has had stock market losses in every year.

By the July 8, 1932 low, the Dow would lose 89.2 percent of its value and its 1929 lofty level of 381.17 would not be surpassed until November 1954, over 25 years later. During the shortest bull market on record the Dow spiked 93.9 percent in 61 days from July to September 1932. Then a five-and-a-half-month relapse brought the Dow back down 37.2 percent on February 27, 1933, just five days before Franklin D. Roosevelt was sworn in as president.

By the time FDR began to implement stimulus programs and financial regulation in 1933 the damage was done, and the country and the world had already plunged into the Great Depression. One of FDR's first orders of business was a nine-day bank moratorium one day after taking office. By the end of March 1933, 12,800 of 18,000 banks had reopened. The United States went off the gold standard in April and passed the Glass-Steagall Act in June, which established the Federal Deposit Insurance Corporation (FDIC) and mandated the separation of commercial banks and investment banks.

Prohibition was repealed in December as the entire country needed a drink. U.S. unemployment reached a peak of 25 percent in 1933 at the depths of the Depression. The reforms continued in 1934 with the creation of the Securities and Exchange Commission and FDR's New Deal programs. A four-year expansion from 1933 to 1937 was only interrupted briefly by a mild five-and-a-half-month bear market in 1934 that clipped a mere 22.8 percent off the Dow, the smallest bear market decline since the seven-month, 18.6 percent mini-bear in 1923.

But as America was rebuilding, totalitarianism was brewing in Europe; and, in Asia, Japan invaded China, the Soviet Union, and Mongolia. In the spring of 1937, a yearlong bear market and recession gripped the United States. European war drums and Wall Street scandals scared investors and FDR's attempts to balance the budget further depressed the economy. From March 1937 to March 1938 the Dow fell 49.1 percent, its third worst bear market decline since 1900. In April 1938, FDR reversed course on balancing the budget and increased spending, which began an expansion that continued through World War II and ended the Great Depression.

World War II

Germany annexed Czechoslovakia in March 1939 and German tanks rolled into Poland on September 1, 1939, signifying the start of World War II. Germany and Italy aligned and Britain and France declared war on Germany. In 1940 Germany invaded Western Europe and France fell in June. Meanwhile, Japan and China waged the Second Sino-Japanese War from October 1938 to December 1941 when Japan bombed Pearl Harbor and joined the Axis Powers while China sided with the Allies.

By the end of 1941, the world was completely at war with the Axis Powers headed by Germany, Japan, and Italy on one side and the Allies led by the British, French, Soviets, Chinese, and U.S. forces on the other. The beginning of WWII caused a three-year losing run for stocks from 1939 to 1941. Once the United States entered the war in force in 1942, the Dow put in its final low of 92.99 on April 28, 1942. The fourth longest bull market would rally the Dow 128.7 percent over the next four years as Allied victories raised spirits and the war machine stimulated the economy.

World War II ended on September 2, 1945, when the Japanese surrendered to the United States. The onset of the war brought rising prices as usual. This resulted in a 74 percent rise in the cost of living between 1941 and 1948. The CPI rose from approximately 42 to 73. Stocks and the economy consolidated over the next three years from mid-1946 to mid-1949 when the next super boom began.

The Consumer Boom

After a post-World War II bear market and recession from mid-1946 to mid-1947, the economy and stock market began to find its footing. The Marshall Plan rebuilt Europe from 1947 to 1951, but the Cold War began as the Truman Doctrine combated Communism. Nevertheless, by 1949 happy days were here again. The post-World War II consumer boom vaulted the economy and stock market higher for the next 16 years on a steady diet of enabling technologies accessible to an expanding middle class as the suburban paradigm shift generated new towns. Meanwhile technological advances made during World War II morphed into new industries. A society that was polarized into urban centers and farms melted into suburban sprawl during the baby boom, and everyone needed a house filled with appliances like TVs, refrigerators, washers, dryers, and the like. Roads were built so folks could commute to their jobs in the big city.

WHY NOT KOREA?

The Korean War was a major international military entanglement that cost the United States over 36,500 lives. It lasted for three years, longer than the U.S. involvement in World War I, but it did not have much effect on the market. The Dow only lost 12 percent over two-and-a-half weeks after North Korea invaded South Korea on June 25, 1950. Then the market resumed its uptrend.

The recent World War II victory and the brutal atomic bomb attack on Japan were fresh in the world's mind, muting the impact of the Korean War on the market. U.S. forces from the Pacific theater of World War II were still in the vicinity so mobilization was less of an undertaking. Leftover World War II materiel was readily available so military spending was lower.

The Korean War did not consume the entire world or U.S. coffers. Inflation was nowhere in sight. The CPI retreated for a year-and-a-half from late 1948 to early 1950 and only increased 13 percent during the war. While tragic and a major U.S. commitment to this day, the Korean War was just a brief pause in the boom of the 1950s and 1960s.

Irrespective of the Cold War, stocks kept rocking and rolling through the 1950s and 1960s. Truman, Eisenhower, JFK, and Martin Luther King Jr. were visionary leaders who inspired the nation. Kennedy's mission to put a man on the moon in less than a decade was successful, using one of the first integrated circuit computers—amazing!

King forged an agenda of equal rights and justice for all people through nonviolent protest that continues today. Urbanization and mass production fueled corporate profits and the Dow sailed 523 percent higher from 1949 to 1966 on a sweeping current of peace, prosperity, spending, and the rise of the new middle class as it caught up with World War II inflation.

The Vietnam War Heats Up Inflation

The Civil Rights Act of 1964 outlawing racial discrimination and segregation passed in July and set off race tensions that would haunt the nation throughout the rest of the 1960s, beginning with riots in New York City later that month. Meanwhile, in response to a naval engagement between North Vietnam and the United States, the Gulf of Tonkin Resolution was approved unanimously on August 7, 1964, by the U.S. Congress and permitted Lyndon B. Johnson the use of conventional military force in Southeast Asia, marking the official beginning of the Vietnam War.

Following Johnson's defeat of Goldwater in the 1964 presidential election, the U.S. escalated bombing in November 1964. Regular bombing began in February 1965 and the first U.S. combat forces arrived in Vietnam on March 8, 1965. A few days later, Federal Reserve Board Chairman William McChesney Martin Jr. warned that the economy was getting close to overheating. The year 1966, the year the Hirsch Organization incorporated and conceived the *Stock Trader's Almanac*, was fraught with peril. In May, U.S. forces commenced firing into Cambodia and the full-blown bombing of Hanoi began on June 29. With geopolitical wrangling on high in Indochina, U.S. forces in the Vietnam theater neared 500,000 by year-end.

Throughout 1967 and 1968 the stock market and the country reacted to Johnson's expansion of the war and the carnage, antiwar protests, riots, and the assassinations of Martin Luther King Jr. and Robert Kennedy. This kept a lid on stock prices and increased war spending, up 50 percent from 1964 to 1968, and began to heat up inflation with the CPI running at an annual rate of 5 percent at the end of 1968. As the market swooned in 1969, the Fed began to fight inflation by increasing prime interest rates to a record high. Neil Armstrong walked on the moon. Some 500,000 hippies gathered at Woodstock. And the draft was reinstated for the first time since World War II.

Protests and demonstrations against the Vietnam War, racism, repression, civil rights for women and minorities, as well as on environmental issues plagued the nation in 1970. U.S. forces entered Cambodia on April 30. Four students were shot and killed by National Guardsmen at a war protest at Kent State University in

Ohio on May 4, and two were killed on May 15 as police fired on a demonstration at Jackson State University in Mississippi. With Wall Street already sour on Richard Nixon's state of the union, this confluence of volatile events in the spring of 1970 drove the Standard & Poor's 500 Index down 25.9 percent in just four-and-a-half months to the midterm bear market bottom on May 26.

Nixon's halt on the convertibility of gold and the implementation of wage and price controls tipped the scales in 1971 and helped push the market lower as the United States bombed North Vietnam heavily. Inflation cranked up. The CPI had climbed 32.3 percent from 93 when the Gulf of Tonkin Resolution passed to 123 at the end of 1971. The prospects for peace and Nixon's reelection pushed the Dow to its war high of 1051.70 on January 11, 1973, which would not be surpassed for 10 years.

Direct U.S. involvement in the Vietnam War officially came to an end on January 27, 1973, with the signing of the Paris Peace Accords. But the war dragged on for two more years. The year 1974, during which Hank Aaron hit homerun 715 to break Babe Ruth's record, was shrouded in turmoil. Even though the Arab oil embargo that began on October 19, 1973, was lifted on March 18, 1974, the damage was already done, causing a severe recession in the United States that would last until 1975.

Watergate scandal hearings and trials got ugly in the spring. To avoid impeachment, Nixon was forced to resign on August 9, 1974, the first U.S. president to do so. Stocks plummeted on the news lopping 23.0 percent off the S&P in less than two months and 27.6 percent off the Dow by December in the final plunge of the 1973 to 1974 bear and the final low of the 1966 to 1982 secular bear. The last Marines evacuated the embassy during the fall of Saigon on April 30, 1975. The *Mayaguez* incident in which the Khmer Rouge hijacked the U.S. merchant container ship the *SS Mayaguez* in May 1975 marked the United States' last official battle of the Vietnam War.

That 1970s Stagflation

When the fireworks smoke had cleared from the bicentennial celebrations and *Viking II* landed on Mars, OPEC increased oil prices again in December 1976. Post-Vietnam War and energy crisis inflation really began to ramp up in 1978. The CPI had jumped 117 percent from 93 in 1964 to 202 in 1978. The Three Mile Island disaster in 1979 unfortunately put a damper on nuclear power in the United States, which could have alleviated much of our energy trials and tribulations back then—and still can.

The 1979 energy crisis began when OPEC raised oil prices on July 15, the same day President Jimmy Carter gave his "crisis of confidence speech" outlining a proposal to reduce U.S. dependence on foreign oil with a 10-year $140 billion program. Gold rallied precipitously as William and Nelson Hunt began their attempt to corner the silver market, and Iran seized the U.S. embassy and took hostages. But the appointment of the caped-inflation-fighter, Paul Volcker, to chairman of the Federal Reserve Board bolstered the economy and the country, limiting the Dow's loss to 16.4 percent during the 17-month bear market from September 1978 to April 1980.

From 1979 through 1981 sky-high inflation, record interest rates, high oil prices, the U.S. boycott of the 1980 Moscow Summer Olympics, economic sanctions on the U.S.S.R. over the invasion of Afghanistan, the Iran hostage crisis, and the Hunt brothers' silver debacle, forced another bear market and recession that would both end in midterm 1982. Gross national product fell 1.8 percent in 1982, the worst decline since 1946. Unemployment reached 10.8 percent in November 1982, its highest level since the Depression.

The Information Revolution

The ancients performed computations and arithmetic processes for thousands of years on tools like the abacus. During the first 2,000 years of the modern era, mechanical computing devices evolved from the astronomical clock to slide rules. According to the *Oxford English Dictionary*, the word "computer" was first used in 1613 to describe "a person who makes calculations or computations."

The paper punch card loom in 1801 led to Herman Hollerith's Tabulating Machine Company in 1896, which became the core of the company that would change its name to International Business Machines (IBM) in 1924. The first electronic computers were developed between 1940 and 1945. IBM and the "Seven Dwarfs" (Burroughs, UNIVAC, NCR, Control Data, Honeywell, RCA, and General Electric) produced mainframes from the late 1950s through the 1970s. But it was not until the 1960s and early 1970s that the seeds of the Internet, the personal computer, and the information age were planted with the development of programmable computer language, packet switching, and integrated circuit microprocessors.

In his book, *A Programming Language*, Kenneth E. Iverson describes how he invented, while at Harvard, the mathematical notations that would later be used in IBM systems when he worked there in the early 1960s. ARPANET and the TCP/IP Internet Protocol were first developed in 1969. When Intel's first general-purpose commercial 4004 microprocessor was shipped in 1971, the roots of the information boom took hold.

Over the next decade the personal computer evolved from Hewlett-Packard's BASIC programmable computer to the Apple IIe, released in January 1983. Microsoft introduced MS-DOS in IBM PCs in 1982 at the same time the stock market launched its stratospheric rise. AOL commenced its dedicated online service in 1985 and the World Wide Web was born in 1992, sending the

BOOM-TIME WAR

Like the Korean War, the Persian Gulf War of 1990 and 1991 was a major international military campaign that was instigated by the unilateral invasion of one country by another. After an unprovoked Iraq took over a sovereign United Nations member nation, a global trade embargo was imposed and Iraq was given until January 15, 1991, to withdraw from Kuwait.

Military intervention was authorized as the United States, NATO, Persian Gulf States, and other nations from around the world amassed nearly 1 million coalition forces around Iraq and Kuwait. The world stood shoulder-to-shoulder in defense of Kuwait. Under then-Chairman of the Joint Chiefs Colin Powell's doctrine of "overwhelming force," Operation Desert Storm was the swiftest, least lethal, and least costly military engagement in U.S. history.

Actual combat operations lasted a mere six weeks with the ground phase taking only four days for the United States and its allies to defeat Iraq and liberate Kuwait on February 27, 1991. While we were all mesmerized by the almost surreal news conferences and video play-by-play of the war by Powell and Coalition Commander General Norman Schwarzkopf, this event had little lasting impact on the economy, market, or inflation.

stock market into outer space. Cellular phones and wireless technology inflated the speculative bubble to the breaking point.

The Greatest Boom

The U.S.S.R. began to break up in early 1990 and the savings and loan crisis came to a close. The longest bull market in history began its historic rise on October 11, 1990, until the Asian currency flu and the collapse of the Russian ruble created a global currency crisis that triggered the shortest bear market on record. The Dow dropped 19.3 percent in 45 days in the summer of 1998. Renowned currency hedge fund, Long-Term Capital Management, is caught in the carnage and the Fed engineered a $3.5 billion bailout.

A double bottom formed in August and October ahead of the final run to the 2000 top. In the final stage of the super bull, tech IPOs and day trading inflated the dotcom stock bubble to epic proportions. During the twentieth century's greatest boom the Dow climbed 1,447 percent from its intraday low on August 11, 1982, at 770 to its intraday high of 11,908.50 on January 14, 2000.

As the boom reached its nadir in late 1999 the core financial regulations that kept the markets a level playing field were dismantled. The Gramm-Leach-Bliley Act of 1999, signed into law by President Clinton on November 12, 1999, repealed key aspects of the Glass-Steagall Act of 1933 that prevented banking, securities, and insurance companies from acting as any combination of an investment bank, commercial bank, and an insurance company. Then the Commodity Futures Modernization Act of 2000 was signed into law on December 21, 2000, also by Wild Bill Clinton, which effectively ensured deregulation of over-the-counter derivatives transactions between sophisticated parties.

These two acts opened the door for the subprime mortgage fiasco, the shadow banking system of collateralized mortgage obligations (CMOs) and credit default swaps (CDSs) and the 2007 to 2009 global financial crisis, recession, and bear market, the aftereffects of which still linger today.

Lather, Rinse, Repeat

So you see we have been there before and have a bureau full of T-shirts to prove it. We may never have seen anything like the 9/11 terrorist attacks that instigated the wars in Afghanistan, Iraq, and on terror, but is it really that much different than the assassination of Archduke Ferdinand in 1914, Pearl Harbor, or the Gulf of Tonkin incident? They are similar random acts of international violence designed to pick a fight.

Financial crises have plagued the turn of the last two centuries, the Depression, and the 1970s. Rampant speculation, unhealthy lax market rules, and a lack of oversight allowed fraud and manipulation to poison the market. But once peacetime arrived, inflation abated, sensible government prevailed, innovation flourished, economies expanded, and the market soared to new heights.

At a Glance

- War and financial crisis are the core elements of economic and market stagnation. Inflation and political ineptitude perpetuate it.
- Peace, price stability, political effectiveness, and innovation ignite and fuel the next long boom and extended market advance.

Chapter Four

The Coming Boom

~

Getting Ready for the Next 500 Percent Move

SUPER BOOMS OF THE past were conceived during wartime and financial crises with pent-up demand, elevated government spending, and mushrooming inflation; weaned on peace, political leadership, and effective governing; then fed a steady diet of cultural paradigm-shifting enabling technology that changed the world and the way the average person on the street lived.

Once major wars ended and the bill came due, inflation peaked. As the inflation rate leveled off years later and financial crises and panic mitigated and the economy began to find some footing, nurtured by pragmatic and progressive government policy and initiatives, new game-changing technologies and ways of life ignited the boom. Heightened consumer spending spurs business and economic growth and the great economist Keynes' "animal spirit" of business, entrepreneurs, and investors is restored, shifting the boom into high gear. Demand for new goods and services generates mounting consumer spending, which puts the boom into overdrive until it reaches critical mass and cruising altitude before falling back to earth.

Unemployment is high, the Great Recession is hardly in the rearview mirror, and global debt is a mounting concern—these are the headlines and newsworthy stories of today. The average investor is saturated with negative news from brokers, family, friends, and government. So my super boom prediction made in May 2010 that the Dow would reach 38,820 by 2025 seemed absurd to many when it was announced. That came as no surprise—all bold predictions are first lambasted before proven true. This super boom is not only plausible but mathematically and historically within reason. Moves of this magnitude have happened several times throughout history, and they have always been preceded by tumultuous times and economic flatlines. In fact, big moves have happened with such regularity and clear cause that we have successfully identified why they happen, how they happen, when they happen, and what to invest in before and as they happen. By examining the past, we are able to shed light on the future.

The first inklings of another potential 500 percent move in the stock market began to materialize in September 2002 as the first major downdraft of the secular bear market, begun in January 2000 with the dot-com crash, came to a close. The war drums were beating to invade Iraq and the stock market was plunging into the midterm elections.

Individual investors remain disenchanted with the stock market, Wall Street pundits, and economists are on either end of the spectrum. The new bull market is under way or Armageddon approaches. However, the writing on the wall is clear. The long secular bear market is in its latter stages. Several more years of healing are before us, but the next super boom is already setting up. High levels of cash are waiting to pour back in and when they do, the all-clear horn blows. The rest of the chapter covers the unfortunate events of the past 12 years and points out which data we need to be watching as harbingers of the coming boom.

Dot-com Bust versus 1929 Crash

March 2009 may have brought new lows to old-school market indices like the Dow and S&P 500, but that was not the case for the tech-laden NASDAQ that nowadays often provides a better picture of the economy and stock market than its blue-chip brethren. Many gloom-and-doomers are predicting new Dow lows in the future. In both 1929 and 2000, a speculative bubble burst and a punishing crash lasting nearly three years took place. Except in 2000, NASDAQ bore the brunt of the carnage while the stodgy, mostly dividend-paying Dow stocks held up better, off only 37.8 percent from January 2000 to October 2002. Similar to the 89.2 percent pounding the Dow took after the 1929 debacle, it was the dotcoms and wireless stocks, plus the few unscrupulous ones using accounting witchcraft, that drove NASDAQ down 77.9 percent. This almost matches—in depth—what occurred 70 years earlier. As for duration, 999 days ending in 2002 on the ninth of bear-killer October is just a month short of matching the length of the "big one" of yesteryear. The Dow received its comeuppance from 2007 to 2009 when all the major averages were cut by more than half. But NASDAQ's 2002 low was not breached, indicating that the wartime secular bear low for the beginning of the twenty-first century is in.

The Global War on Terror

The onset of the global war on terror and the Iraq and Afghanistan wars was September 11, 2001, when the World Trade Center and the Pentagon were attacked by terrorists. In response, U.S. forces attacked terrorist strongholds in Afghanistan on October 7. Then on March 20, 2003, air bombardment of Iraq started. U.S. forces marched into Baghdad in short order and President Bush announced the "Mission Accomplished" in May 2003, but that would not be the case. Nevertheless, stocks rallied like it was 1999 with the Dow gaining 43.5 percent from the October 9, 2002, midterm year low to the preelection year high on the last day of 2003. NASDAQ was up 50.0 percent for calendar year 2003. The consecutive gains in preelection years since 1939 would continue. As the war dragged on over the next two years the Dow held the 10,500 line. Then the credit and housing bubble inflated on equal parts deregulation, lax oversight, predatory lending practices, and shadow banking.

Bubblicious Housing

The housing market was at the heart of the financial crisis. The inflation and subsequent bursting of the housing bubble was a seminal event in the history of Wall Street and will be a topic analyzed and debated for generations. Let's put the situation in perspective. Bubbles are usually self-evident, especially in retrospect. It was easy to quantify the tech bubble; NASDAQ ran up to 5,048 and crashed to 1,114. It is easily discernible on any long-term NASDAQ chart. The housing situation was not as cut and dried. The main reason the general public was blindsided by the housing market is that there is no high-profile metric to gauge the relative level.

The housing bubble formed for several reasons. Some contend that the origin was the overly aggressive monetary policy in the wake of 9/11 where the Fed's target rate was held at ridiculously low levels (under 2 percent) for the better part of three years. Others point to nefarious lending practices and a gullible populace. Reality is somewhere in between. But what is it going to take to fix a problem that most people cannot identify? What will the recovery look like?

Greed, hubris, irresponsibility, and foolishness on the part of the lenders and the borrowers caused it. Despite the propensity to lay blame, it all does not fall on Wall Street and the banks. No one forced people to buy a house they could not afford. No one made homeowners treat their houses like live-in ATMs. This country was founded on a strong fiscal ethic of saving; we all lost our way! Until the housing market is fixed, the economy is in hot water. The magnitude of the damage was far beyond what anyone envisioned.

Recently there has been a fair amount of media buzz (again) about a housing market recovery. Sure, sentiment and sales figures have improved recently, but according to four key pieces of housing data that we track: existing home sales, housing starts, new home sales, and the National Association of Home Builders' (NAHB) Housing Market Index (HMI), the reported recovery does not look all that impressive. Much of the bleeding has stopped, but a great deal of healing is still needed for the housing market to once again become a healthy component of the economy. A sustained rise in these four indicators will help us know when the economy is once again on sure footing:

- **Existing home sales:** Existing home sales is the single most important piece of data that affects individuals. It is a measure of the ease in which one can buy and sell a house and reflects the relative value that your house has. The massive crescendo in 2006 is indicative of just how out of whack the market got. Not only were people buying houses that they shouldn't have, but individuals were flipping houses for a quick buck. When 7 million houses were changing hands each year, something was wrong. The 2006 data should have set off alarms on Pennsylvania Avenue.

Existing home sales were a relatively stable number until 1996. There were swings, but relatively minor, after all, a family home is a long-term investment. Existing home sales have leveled off recently, but we are far from out of the woods. Many homes have been sold at considerable losses or foreclosed upon. This number has vacillated wildly since its 2005 peak with a downward trend. Sales spiked in 2009 and again in 2010 on home-buyer tax credits, but those credits have since expired. When existing homes sales finally stabilize in a realistic range, the bottom should be set.

- **Housing starts:** Housing starts are indicative of how builders feel about the housing market, and are important for two reasons. First, home building provides a lot of jobs. When new home building sours, whole construction crews are out of work. Second, housing starts are a leading indicator of the amount of risk that the market is willing to take. In a good market, home builders ramp up construction in anticipation of future sales. When the market turns they quickly rein in their plans.

From the housing bottom in 1991 to the top in 2006, housing starts jumped from under 800,000 to over 2,270,000 on an annualized basis, a number not seen since 1972. Since the top, the number of housing starts crumbled back below 500,000 in 2009 and is currently looking for support above that level. This is a function of weak demand and restrictive lending requirements despite historically low interest rates. With a frozen credit market, builders cannot borrow money to buy land and material and finance payroll. Although they seem to have stabilized, housing starts will be one of the first indicators to foreshadow the recovery.

- **New home sales:** It takes longer to build a house than sell a house, resulting in a buildup of inventory. Homebuilders attempt to strike a balance and plan their new construction accordingly. New home sales fell off of a cliff—down 80 percent from almost 1,400,000 to 280,000 in the five years from 2005 to 2010 and currently are not much higher. The glut of new homes continues to depress home prices and restrict new construction jobs. New home sales will be the last indicator to turn, but will provide an important confirmation when the housing market has fully healed.

- **Housing Market Index:** The National Association of Home Builders (NAHB) Housing Market Index (HMI) may be the best indicator for judging the overall health of the housing market. The HMI was ahead of the curve in forecasting the imminent demise of the market. From 2005 to 2006, th HMI leveled off and turned down well befo the other data began to crumble. The HMI wi also convey any optimism within the industry before the data confirms a recovery. Numbers above 5 are a positive bias, below is negative. The inde has hovered below 20 since 2007. Upticks over th past two years have been encouraging but pro fleeting. The big swings have been fake outs, sho ing that the HMI cannot be looked at in a vacuum Nonetheless, it is an early warning for swings in the housing market in both directions. It is a number that should be monitored closely.

Epic damage was done to the economy. It is going to take a concerted effort to repair it and instill confidence among homebuilders, banks, and the American public. Housing led us down the primrose path and it will also help lead us out of this mess. Monitor these four numbers closely and you will have a good idea of where the economy (and the market) is, and more importantly where they are going. Until housing recovers there is no chance for a meaningful or sustainable bull market to emerge.

Credit markets have begun to thaw and builders are borrowing money to buy land and material and finance payroll as housing starts are now dancing with an annualized rate of 700,000. Housing starts have stabilized, but still remain below the lows of the previous three decades. This is an indication that the multiyear healing process that sets the stage for the next super boom is likely under way. New home sales continue to scrape the bottom of the graph. A consistently increasing number of new home sales will be one of the last signposts of the coming boom. Existing home sales and the HMI have shown the greatest signs of life recently. The HMI's recent break above 20 is encouraging but still well shy of 50.

Four Horsemen of the Economy

International terrorism, Iraq and Afghanistan, Iran and North Korea, the Arab Spring, the housing market, job creation, decay of our once-great infrastructure, and our shamefully expensive and inefficient health care system are some of the issues that plague this still-great country and society. Each must be dealt with, but the paramount topic, the one that will cascade throughout the entire globe is this: What is to become of the great American economy? The engine that has fueled the globe since the Second World War is in dire need of an overhaul.

Though we appear to have weathered the mother of all financial crises and the Great Recession, much has remained unchanged in the way this country conducts its business. Americans remain unhappy with the status quo. After a prosperous two-and-a-half decades we are on the precipice of regressing back to the not-so-super 1970s. Quite frankly, the economic situation in this country is still a bummer. Lofty ideas on how to make the U.S. economy better such as green-collar jobs, strengthening the middle class, comprehensive government reform, and changing the tax codes have not materialized. If the economy continues to sour, new leadership will be installed in Washington on both ends of Pennsylvania Avenue.

There is no shortage of dire predictions for the near term in the United States. There are also many well-respected economists whose conclusions are not nearly as ominous. Either current policy is sufficient with a tweak here and there, or economic policy must be revamped. The Four Horsemen of the Economy, the Dow, consumer confidence, inflation, and unemployment are common data points that quickly and simply gauge the economy. Individually they indicate different aspects of strength in the U.S. economy; collectively they provide a rather complete picture.

1. **The Dow:** Even the most ardent Dow theorist would confess the index is not without its limitations.

The S&P is far broader and, thanks to constant rebalancing, reflects current trends. The NASDAQ is a much better indicator of innovation and growth. But as a barometer for gauging the health of corporate America, the Dow is nonpareil. When the Dow is doing well, the United States is doing well; when the Dow is in a funk, it not only ripples throughout Wall Street, but Main Street as well. The biggest impact is felt by investors, generally members of the upper-middle class and above—those with 401(k)s, bonuses, mutual funds, and/or investment portfolios.

2. **Consumer confidence:** The Consumer Confidence Index is essentially a proxy for the middle class's belief in the economy. The middle class in this country has been squeezed for the better part of the past two decades. Consumer confidence is all about perception and expectations. It is a referendum on the economy of Main Street. The burst of stimulus has helped rejuvenate confidence, but readings around 70 indicate U.S. middle class consumers remain fatigued and strapped for cash. Retail spending has picked up, but from severely depressed levels. Until the Con-Con Index heads back up toward 90, as it did in the early 1980s, we do not expect a sustainable recovery.

3. **Inflation:** Inflation hits American small to mid-sized business owners and the little guy hardest. Generally upper-middle to lower-upper, the small business owner is the backbone of this country. Small business employs tens of millions of Americans. If small businesses are not doing well, it spills over to huge swaths of the populace. Sustained levels of super high inflation have always created economic problems. Extreme deflation is also an economic depressant.

As measured by the Producer Price Index (PPI) and the Consumer Price Index (CPI), inflation is on the rise. At this juncture of the recovery this is a good thing. This is the beginning of the inflation that will catapult the economy and the stock market into the next boom. At some point inflation will need to abate or the economy will overheat. That is not likely to happen for several years, but it will at some point down the line as it has in the past. Like everyone else, the Fed and other economic policy makers are not perfect and will likely overshoot on accommodative monetary policy as they have many times before. The lag and complexity of the data makes it difficult to perfectly time changes in monetary policy.

4. **Unemployment:** Unemployment is the ultimate arbitrator of the middle class in times of economic

turmoil. In times of serious economic instability, unemployment seeps all the way to upper management. The jobs situation in this country unraveled to a level not seen since the double-dip recession days of the early 1980s. But it is not simply the absolute level that is important. The trend of an increasing or decreasing number of Americans working also matters. The unemployment rate has receded from crisis levels, but the recent uptick is concerning. Not until we see a sustained retreat will the economy be on the path to real recovery and higher growth rates.

Economic conditions are improving slowly and moderately in fits and starts. The labor market has shown signs of life and housing has also shown a pulse lately, but after a few months of improvement the data steps back. The Dow continues to move sideways as it has since the summer of 1998. Consumer confidence has improved since the depths of the Great Recession, but it turned down quickly in 2011 as trouble began to brew in Washington and the economic expansion decelerated. Inflation is on the rise with the CPI back up to 3 percent annually after being negative for much of 2009 and up 29 percent since 2001. Unemployment has been stubborn, but is finally trending significantly lower. It may rise again before this secular bear goes into hibernation.

The Colt of the Economy

In protracted, long-term bear markets as we have been in since 2000, job creation is the "colt of the economy," or the lynchpin to recovery. The official unemployment rate is a lagging indicator, peaking on average nine months after the end of the bear market and on occasion a year or more later. Initial jobless claims is a somewhat less lagging unemployment metric. This weekly gauge cuts out much of the government's statistical shenanigans and simply measures folks filing for unemployment insurance for the first time.

Recessionary bear market bottoms are usually within two months of the peak in initial jobless claims, except for one. Since 1967, initial jobless claims have peaked, on average, about one month after the bear market bottom during a recession. Only the October 1990 bottom induced by Iraq's invasion of Kuwait had initial jobless claims peak more than two months later. Claims topped out five months later in March 1991 when coalition forces ousted Saddam Hussein's forces from Kuwait. Initial jobless claims peaked and reversed course in late March 2009, three weeks after the low. It indicated the bear market was over and the continued retreat shows an economy on the mend. This metric may be prone to spikes over the next several years as it was during long recovery from 1974 to 1984.

We're Not There Yet

The low point of the economy and the bottom of the stock market appear to be behind us. But other factors have yet to align. CPI has risen just 29 percent since October 2001. President Obama has tried to tack to the center, but we have yet to see him exhibit unwavering leadership and inspire the country. If the new Republican leadership in Congress and the White House can't get the country rolling again, new leaders with new ideas will be voted in and a properly functioning federal government will evolve over the next eight years.

Communication and connectivity have helped bring the four corners of the world into greater harmony. But troublesome hot spots still exist—not just in places like North Korea, the Near East, the Middle East, sub-Saharan Africa, Haiti, and so on, but right here in the cities and towns across America. Since the birth of the United States of America, the first truly representational government and free market system, planet Earth has been on an increasingly stable path of growth, peace, equal rights, and justice. As we have learned to master much of the rest of our environment, we have learned to stabilize the swings of expansion and contraction, speculation and investment, innovation and growth, and international power struggles.

True it has been crazy these past 30 years. We've endured the super boom of all time in the 1980s and 1990s followed by 9/11, a protracted war on several fronts, asset and debt bubbles, financial crises, market crashes (flash and otherwise), and the Great Recession. But by my reckoning it's been better than past demises. I have not had to wait on a gasoline line in the twenty-first century, on odd and even license-plate-rationing days as I did as a child in late 1973 and early 1974 and again in 1979.

The 1982 to 2000 super boom was one of a kind, powered by baby boomer consumerism and incredible technological advancement. It will be a hard act to follow. The post-World War I and World War II booms were warm-up acts. There was no baby boom to power them, but waves of immigrants helped create plenty of demand and an appetite for a better life through new ideas and hard work. Many of the innovations of the 1980s and 1990s were spawned in the first 80 years of the twentieth century and earlier. But nonetheless, the breakthroughs of previous generations took the economy, society, and stocks to new heights.

The future may look bleak now, but as John D. Rockefeller accurately said in July 1932 on his 93rd birthday, "Depressions have come and gone. Prosperity has always returned and will again." We have experienced economic and fiscal challenges before and will ride out of it again on the back of political stability, reduced global violence, inflation, human ingenuity, and the zest for life!

Inflation alone cannot trigger a boom. A new innovation or technological breakthrough is needed. Henry Ford spawned mass production in the 1920s. World War II triggered a baby boom and the suburbanization of the United States, plus aviation developments substantially shrunk the size of the planet. And from the ashes of the 1970s stagflation the microprocessor was born, eventually giving rise to the personal computer, the Internet, and a global communications infrastructure capable of nearly any feat.

Our aging population is not a handicap; it is an opportunity. Biotech and pharmaceutical companies know this and are working night and day to meet the needs of this demographic. Personal electronics are hungry for power and as a society we are becoming increasingly aware of the detrimental effects of hydrocarbon use. Cheap, clean, and renewable energy will be in demand.

Exogenous events will occur that could accelerate or delay the Dow's arrival at 38,820. The supercollider in Europe could unlock unknown secrets well ahead of schedule. Believe me, scientists are just as eager as the next to capitalize on their hard work. Great inventions and solutions to modern problems could be unearthed any day. Terrorists may also, to everyone's chagrin, have a successful moment. These events cannot be forecast with any degree of certainty. However, many millennia of human nature and triumph over adversity are worth betting at least a portion of your retirement nest egg on. A Dow Jones Industrial Average of 38,820 by 2025 is not a market forecast; it is an expectation that human ingenuity will overcome adversity, just as it has on countless past occasions.

Five Years to Go

Figure 4.1 visually portrays my long-term forecast, which projects a continuing sideways market through the year

Figure 4.1   Thirteen-Year Projection

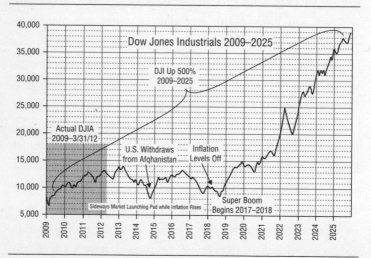

2017 or 2018 with the Dow remaining in a range of roughly 7,000 to 14,000 before it takes off and completes a 500 percent move from the intraday low of 6,470 on March 6, 2009, to 38,820 by the year 2025.

The calculus behind this forecast includes the disengagement of the U.S. military combat operations from entrenched overseas wars. Rising inflation from massive government spending and easy monetary policy over the next 5 to 10 years will begin to taper off as the stock market begins to inflate sixfold. And finally, technological innovations from alternative energy, biotechnology, or other yet-to-be-discovered fields will enable a cultural paradigm shift across the planet that will fuel exponential growth as the automobile, television, microprocessor, Internet, and cell phone have done in the past. To wit: War and Peace + Inflation + Secular Bull Market + Enabling Technology = 500% Super Boom Move.

In order to create this chart I relied on the market's behavior and global economic trends during the last three major boom-and-bust cycles of the twentieth century revolving around the three major wars (World War I, World War II, and Vietnam), as well as the monthly, seasonal, annual, and four-year cycle trends during the flat-bust periods and the rising-boom periods.

The Dow is expected to test 10,000 again. Then, after stalling near 14,000-resistance in 2012–2013, Dow

8,000 is likely to come under fire in 2013–2014 as we withdraw from Afghanistan. Resistance will likely be met in 2015–2017 near 13,000 to 14,000. Another test of 8,000-support in 2017–2018 is expected as inflation begins to level off and the next super boom commences. By 2020, we should be testing 15,000 and after a brief pullback be on our way to 25,000 in 2022. A bear market in midterm 2022 should be followed by a three- to four-year tear toward Dow 40,000.

At a Glance

- U.S. military engagement overseas will continue to stifle economic prosperity and the market.
- Prevailing peace will inspire the government and private sector to conspire together, stimulating innovation and economic growth.
- Signposts from housing, employment, the Dow, consumers, and inflation will herald the commencement of the next super boom.

Chapter Five

Your Portfolio
Gets Political

*How the Presidential Election
Cycle Impacts the Markets*

WHAT HAPPENS ON WALL STREET in inextricably linked to what transpires in Washington. For five decades, the *Stock Trader's Almanac* has discussed—and demonstrated—the importance of the four-year presidential election/stock market cycle. The four-year cycle is the "Old Faithful" of indicators for us.

Don't get me wrong. I am a strong proponent of historical and seasonal market patterns, but also fully aware that history never repeats exactly. History has been a guide for navigating current market conditions and predicting significant future trends with quite a degree of reliability over the years. What we try to get *Almanac* investors to do is not necessarily follow historical patterns to a "T" but to keep them in mind so they know when their radar should perk up.

How the Government Manipulates the Economy to Stay in Power

Presidential elections have a profound impact on the economy and the stock market. Wars, recessions, and bear markets tend to start or occur in the first half of a presidential term; prosperous times and bull markets, in the latter half. The greatest gains can be noticed in the third years with weakness in the first two years.

This pattern is most compelling. The entire four-year pattern back to Andrew Jackson's first administration is detailed in Figure 5.1. It is no coincidence that the last two years (preelection year and election year) of the 44 administrations since 1833 produced a total net market gain of 724.0 percent. This gain dwarfs the 273.1 percent gain of the first two years of these administrations.

Figure 5.1   Four-Year Presidential Election Annual % Change in Dow Jones Industrial Average (1833–2011)

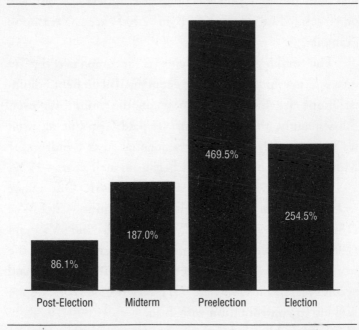

Based on annual close; Prior to 1886 based on Cowles and other indexes; 12 Mixed Stocks, 10 Rails, 2 Industrials 1886–1889; 20 Mixed Stocks, 18 Rails, 2 Inds 1890–1896; Railroad average 1897 (first industrial average published May 26, 1896).

In an effort to gain reelection, presidents tend to take care of most of their more painful initiatives in the first half of their term and prime the pump in the second half so the electorate is most prosperous when they enter the voting booths. A good number of these midterm bottoms occur during the worst six months. After nine straight annual Dow gains from 1992 to 1999 during the millennial bull, the four-year election cycle appears to be back on track. The years 2001 to 2004 are a textbook example.

The making of presidents is accompanied by an unsubtle manipulation of the economy. Incumbent administrations are duty-bound to retain the reins of power. Subsequently, the "piper must be paid," producing what we have coined the "Post-Presidential Year Syndrome." Most big, bad bear markets began in such years—1929, 1937, 1957, 1969, 1973, 1977, and 1981. Our major wars also began in years following elections—Civil War (1861), WWI (1917), WWII (1941), and Vietnam (1965). Post-election 2001 combined with 2002 for the worst back-to-back years since 1973 to1974 (also first and second years). Plus, we had 9/11, the war on terror, and the buildup to confrontation with Iraq.

Some cold, hard facts to prove economic manipulation appeared in a book by Edward R. Tufte called *Political Control of the Economy*. Stimulative fiscal measures designed to increase per capita disposable income, providing a sense of well-being to the voting public, included: increases in federal budget deficits, government spending, and social security benefits; interest rate reductions on government loans; and speedups of projected funding:

Federal Spending: During 1962 to 1973, the average increase was 29 percent higher in election years than in nonelection years.

Social Security: There were nine increases during the 1952 to 1974 period. Half of the six election-year increases became effective in September eight weeks before Election Day. The average increase was 100 percent higher in presidential than in midterm election years.

Real Disposable Income: Accelerated in all but one election year between 1947 and 1973 (excluding the Eisenhower years). Only one of the remaining odd-numbered years (1973) showed a marked acceleration.

These moves were obviously not coincidences and explain why we tend to have a political (four-year) stock market cycle.

Under Ronald Reagan, we paid the piper in 1981 and 1982, followed by eight straight years of expansion. However, we ran up a larger deficit than the total deficit of the previous 200 years of our national existence.

Alan Greenspan took over the Fed from Paul Volker August 11, 1987, and was able to keep the economy rolling until an exogenous event in the Persian Gulf pushed us into a real recession in August 1990, which lasted long enough to choke off the Bush reelection effort in 1992. Three other incumbents in this century failed to retain power: Taft in 1912 when the Republican Party split in two; Hoover in 1932 in the depths of the Great Depression; and Carter in 1980 during the Iran hostage crisis.

Bill Clinton presided for two terms over the incredible economic expansion and market gains of the 1990s. Mr. Clinton was keen to have former Goldman Sachs chief, Robert Rubin, run the Treasury for a stretch, helping his administration create a smooth and beneficial relationship with Wall Street, Main Street, and the Fed.

George W. Bush adeptly navigated the country through recession, the most excruciating bear market since the 1970s, and military action in the first two years of his first administration (2001–2002). Quick initial success in Iraq and major tax cuts, including a bone to Wall Street in a dividend tax cut, helped stimulate the economy and the stock market in preelection year 2003. Low interest rates of his first term and continued deregulation would eventually fuel a credit bubble that would propel the market to new all-time highs (DJIA and S&P 500) in preelection 2007.

Barack Obama took office as financial crisis gripped the world's markets, and during the worst recession since the Great Depression and the second worst bear market since 1900. Record fiscal and monetary stimulus was deployed to combat the recession and its effects. The four-year presidential election cycle was trumped by crisis and recovery efforts, but by 2010 its influence was being felt again.

Political gridlock can be good for the markets, but does it matter if a president is a Democrat or a Republican? There are six possible scenarios on Capitol Hill: Republican president with a Republican Congress, Republican president with a Democratic Congress, Republican president with a split Congress, Democratic president with a Democratic Congress, Democratic president with a Republican Congress, and a Democratic president with a split Congress.

First looking at just the historical performance of the Dow under the Democratic and Republican presidents, we see a pattern that is contrary to popular belief. Under a Democrat, the Dow has performed much better than under a Republican. The Dow has historically returned 10.0 percent under the Democrats compared to a 6.8 percent return under a Republican executive.

The results are the opposite with a Republican Congress, yielding an average 16.8 percent gain in the Dow compared to a 6.1 percent return when the Democrats have control of the Hill.

With total Republican control of Washington, the Dow has been up on average 14.1 percent. Democrats in power over the two branches have fared worse with 7.4

Figure 5.2   Market Performance under Different Political Alignments

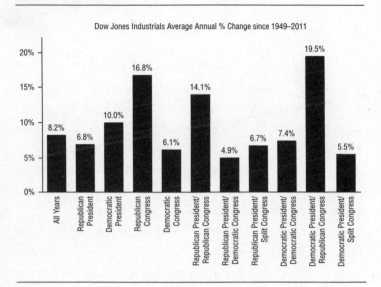

Dow Jones Industrials Average Annual % Change since 1949–2011

percent gains. When power is split, with a Republican president and a Democratic Congress, the Dow has not done very well, averaging only a 6.7 percent gain. The best scenario for all investors is a Democrat in the White House and Republican control of Congress with average gains of 19.5 percent. The direst of circumstance occurs with a Republican president and a Democratic Congress, averaging just 4.9 percent. The Dow's 33.8 percent loss in 2008 is a major factor. See Figure 5.2.

Post-Election-Year Syndrome: Paying the Piper

Politics being what it is, incumbent administrations during election years try to make the economy look good to impress the electorate and tend to put off unpopular decisions until the votes are counted. This produces an American phenomenon—the post-election-year syndrome. The year begins with an inaugural ball, after which the piper must be paid, and we Americans have often paid dearly in the past 99 years.

Victorious candidates rarely succeed in fulfilling campaign promises of "peace and prosperity." In the past 25 post-election years, three major wars began: World War I (1917), World War II (1941), and Vietnam (1965); four drastic bear markets started in 1929, 1937, 1969, and 1973. The terrorist attacks of 9/11, a recession, and a continuing bear market plagued 2001. Global financial calamity and the Great Recession sent the second worst bear market for the Dow to its ultimate low in 2009. Less severe bear markets occurred or were in progress in 1913, 1917, 1921, 1941, 1949, 1953, 1957, 1977, and 1981. Only in 1925, 1989, 1993, and 1997 were Americans blessed with peace and prosperity (see Table 5.1).

Republicans took back the White House following foreign involvements under the Democrats in 1921 (World War I), 1953 (Korea), 1969 (Vietnam), and 1981 (Iran); and a scandal (2001). Bear markets occurred during all or part of these post-election years.

Table 5.1   Post-Election Year Record Since 1913

Year	President	Result
1913	Wilson (D)	Minor bear market.
1917	Wilson (D)	World War I and a bear market.
1921	Harding (R)	Post-war depression and bear market.
1925	Coolidge (R)	Peace and prosperity. Hallelujah!
1929	Hoover (R)	Worst market crash in history.
1933	Roosevelt (D)	Devaluation, bank failures, Depression still on but market strong.
1937	Roosevelt (D)	Another crash, 20% unemployment rate.
1941	Roosevelt (D)	World War II and a continuing bear.
1945	Roosevelt (D)	Post-war industrial contraction, strong market precedes 1946 crash.
1949	Truman (D)	Minor bear market.
1953	Eisenhower (R)	Minor post-war (Korea) bear market.
1957	Eisenhower (R)	Major bear market.
1961	Kennedy (D)	Bay of Pigs fiasco, strong market precedes 1962 crash.
1965	Johnson (D)	Vietnam escalation. Bear came in 1966.
1969	Nixon (R)	Start of worst bear market since 1937.
1973	Nixon, Ford (R)	Start of worst bear market since 1929.
1977	Carter (D)	Bear market in blue chip stocks.
1981	Reagan (R)	Bear strikes again.
1985	Reagan (R)	No bear in sight.
1989	Bush (R)	Effect of 1987 Crash wears off.
1993	Clinton (D)	S&P up 7.1%, next year off 1.5%.
1997	Clinton (D)	S&P up 31.0%, next year up 26.7%.
2001	Bush, GW (R)	9/11, recession, bear market intensifies.
2005	Bush, GW (R)	Flat year, narrowest range, Dow off –0.6%.
2009	Obama (D)	Financial crisis bear market bottom in March.

Democrats recaptured power after domestic problems under the Republicans in 1913 (GOP split in two), 1933 (crash and depression), 1961 (recession), 1977 (Watergate), 1993 (sluggish economy), and 2009 (financial crisis). Democratic post-election years after resuming power were bearish following a Republican Party squabble or scandal and bullish following bad economic times.

Looking at the past you can see that when Democrats ousted Republican White House occupants the market fared better in post-election years than when the reverse occurred. In the past, Democrats came to power over domestic issues and Republicans won the White House on foreign shores.

Wilson won after the Republican Party split in two, and Carter after the Watergate scandal. Roosevelt, Kennedy, and Clinton won elections during bad economies. The Republicans took over after major wars were begun under Democrats, benefiting Harding, Eisenhower, and Nixon. The Iranians made Jimmy Carter appear helpless, which favored Reagan. With no recession and no embarrassing foreign entanglement, the major advantage for Bush was the Clinton scandal. A disjointed Democratic Party and "wartime president" status helped George W. Bush hold the White House in 2004. Financial crisis and the worst recession in generations ushered Obama into the White House in 2008.

Also worth noting is that since 1913 the Dow has dropped –20.9 percent on average from its post-election-year high to its subsequent low in the following midterm year.

Midterm Election Years: Where Bottom Pickers Find Paradise

American presidents have danced the Quadrennial Quadrille over the past two centuries. After the midterm congressional election and the invariable seat loss by his party, the president during the next two years jiggles fiscal policies to get federal spending, disposable income, and social security benefits up and interest rates and inflation down. By Election Day, he will have danced his way into the wallets and hearts of the electorate and, hopefully, will have choreographed four more years in the White House for his party.

When the campaigning and the victory lap are over and the governing begins, the market tends to retreat. Practically all bear markets began and ended in the two years after presidential elections. Bottoms often occurred in an air of crisis: the Cuban Missile Crisis in 1962, tight money in 1966, Cambodia in 1970, Watergate and Nixon's resignation in 1974, and threat of international monetary collapse in 1982. But crisis often creates opportunity in the stock market. In the last 13 quadrennial cycles since 1961, 9 of the 16 bear markets bottomed in the midterm year (see Table 5.2).

Table 5.2   Midterm Election Year Record Since 1914

Year	President	Result
1914	Wilson (D)	Bottom in July. War closed markets.
1918	Wilson (D)	Bottom 12 days prior to start of year.
1922	Harding (R)	Bottom $4^1/_2$ months prior to start of year.
1926	Coolidge (R)	Only drop (7 weeks, −17%) ends March 30.
1930	Hoover (R)	'29 Crash continues through 1930. No bottom.
1934	Roosevelt (D)	First Roosevelt bear, Feb. to July 26 bottom (−23%).
1938	Roosevelt (D)	Big 1937 break ends in March, DJIA off 49%.
1942	Roosevelt (D)	World War II bottom in April.
1946	Truman (D)	Market tops in May, bottoms in October.
1950	Truman (D)	June 1949 bottom, June 1950 Korean War outbreak causes 14% drop.
1954	Eisenhower (R)	September 1953 bottom, then straight up.
1958	Eisenhower (R)	October 1957 bottom, then straight up.
1962	Kennedy (D)	Bottoms in June and October.
1966	Johnson (D)	Bottom in October.
1970	Nixon (R)	Bottom in May.
1974	Nixon, Ford (R)	December Dow bottom, S&P bottom in October.
1978	Carter (D)	March bottom, despite October massacre later.
1982	Reagan (R)	Bottom in August.
1986	Reagan (R)	No bottom in 1985 or 1986.
1990	Bush (R)	Bottom October 11 (Kuwaiti invasion).
1994	Clinton (D)	Bottom April 4 after 10% drop.
1998	Clinton (D)	October 8 bottom (Asian currency crisis, hedge fund debacle).
2002	Bush, GW (R)	October 9 bottom (corporate malfeasance, terrorism, Iraq).
2006	Bush, GW (R)	No Bottom in 2006 (Iraq success, credit bubble).
2010	Obama (D)	March 2009 bottom, then straight up.

Normally, major corrections occur sometime in the first or second years following presidential elections. In the last 13 midterm election years, bear markets began or were in progress 9 times—we experienced bull years in 1986, 2006, and 2010, while 1994 was flat.

The puniest midterm advance, 14.5 percent from the 1946 low, was during the industrial contraction after World War II. The next four smallest advances were: 1978 (OPEC–Iran) 21.0 percent, 1930 (economic collapse) 23.4 percent, 1966 (Vietnam) 26.7 percent, and 2010 (European debt) 32.3 percent.

Since 1914 the Dow has gained 48.6 percent on average from its midterm election year low to its subsequent high in the following preelection year. A swing of such magnitude is equivalent to a move from 10,000 to 15,000 or from 13,000 to 19,500 (see Table 5.3).

Preelection Years: No Dow Losers Since 1939

There hasn't been a down year for the Dow in the third year of a presidential term since war-torn 1939, when the Dow was off 2.9 percent. The only severe loss in a prepresidential election year going back 100 years occurred in 1931 during the Depression.

Electing a president every four years has set in motion a political stock market cycle. Most bear markets take place in the first or second years after elections. Then,

Table 5.3   Dow's Percent Change from Midterm Low to Preelection High

	Midterm Year Low		Preelection Year High		
	Date of Low	Dow	Date of High	Dow	% Gain
1	Jul 30, 1914*	52.32	Dec 27, 1915	99.21	89.6
2	Jan15, 1918**	73.38	Nov 3, 1919	119.62	63.0
3	Jan 10, 1922**	78.59	Mar 20, 1923	105.38	34.1
4	Mar 30, 1926*	135.20	Dec 31, 1927	202.40	49.7
5	Dec 16, 1930*	157.51	Feb 24, 1931	194.36	23.4
6	Jul 26, 1934*	85.51	Nov 19, 1935	148.44	73.6
7	Mar 31, 1938*	98.95	Sep 12, 1939	155.92	57.6
8	Apr 28, 1942*	92.92	Jul 14, 1943	145.82	56.9
9	Oct 9, 1946	163.12	Jul 24, 1947	186.85	14.5
10	Jan 13, 1950**	196.81	Sep 13, 1951	276.37	40.4
11	Jan 11, 1954**	279.87	Dec 30, 1955	488.40	74.5
12	Feb 25, 1958**	436.89	Dec 31, 1959	679.36	55.5
13	Jun 26, 1962*	535.74	Dec 18, 1963	767.21	43.2
14	Oct 7, 1966*	744.32	Sep 25, 1967	943.08	26.7
15	May 26, 1970*	631.16	Apr 28, 1971	950.82	50.6
16	Dec 6, 1974*	577.60	Jul 16, 1975	881.81	52.7
17	Feb 28, 1978*	742.12	Oct 5, 1979	897.61	21.0
18	Aug 12, 1982*	776.92	Nov 29, 1983	1287.20	65.7
19	Jan 22, 1986	1502.29	Aug 25, 1987	2722.42	81.2
20	Oct 11, 1990*	2365.10	Dec 31, 1991	3168.84	34.0
21	Apr 4, 1994	3593.35	Dec 13, 1995	5216.47	45.2
22	Aug 31, 1998*	7539.07	Dec 31, 1999	11497.12	52.5
23	Oct 9, 2002*	7286.27	Dec 31, 2003	10453.92	43.5
24	Jan 20, 2006	10667.39	Oct 9, 2007	14164.53	32.8
25	Jul 2, 2010**	9686.48	Apr 29, 2011	12810.54	32.3
				Average	**48.6%**

*Bear market ended.
**Bear previous year.

the market improves. What happens is that each administration usually does everything in its power to juice up the economy so that voters are in a positive mood at election time. Just take a look at Table 5.4.

Election Year Perspectives and Observations

If I could predict the outcome of the fourth-year presidential election 12 to 18 months ahead of time, it sure would provide insight as to what the market might do during election years. As I can't, I added up the 17 times since 1900 that parties retained the White House and find the Dow gained 15.3 percent in the average election year. The 11 other times "ins" were ousted the Dow lost 4.4 percent on average.

George W. Bush is the first president who failed to win the popular vote to win a second term. John Quincy Adams, a son of a former president, and Benjamin Harrison both failed in their bids for reelection. Rutherford B. Hayes chose not to run in 1880.

Presidential popularity during wartime often fades by the time the war ends, or seems to be ending, and the next presidential election rolls around. The Democrats lost power after WWI (1920), Korea (1952), and Vietnam (1968); the Republicans gave up the White House in 1992, despite their very high ratings during and after Desert Storm. (Even the greatest leader of the century,

Table 5.4   Preelection Year Record Since 1915

Year	President	Result
1915	Wilson (D)	World War I in Europe, but Dow up 81.7%.
1919	Wilson (D)	Post-Armistice 45.5% gain through Nov. 3 top. Dow +30.5%.
1923	Harding/Coolidge (R)	Teapot Dome scandal a depressant. Dow loses 3.3%.
1927	Coolidge (R)	Bull market rolls on, up 28.8%.
1931	Hoover (R)	Depression, stocks slashed in half. Dow −52.7%, S&P −47.1%.
1935	Roosevelt (D)	Almost straight up year, S&P 500 up 41.2%, Dow 38.5%.
1939	Roosevelt (D)	War clouds, Dow −2.9% but 23.7% April-Dec. gain. S&P −5.5%.
1943	Roosevelt (D)	U.S. at war, prospects brighter, S&P +19.4%, Dow +13.8%.
1947	Truman (D)	S&P unchanged, Dow up 2.2%.
1951	Truman (D)	Dow +14.4%, S&P +16.5%.
1955	Eisenhower (R)	Dow +20.8%, S&P +26.4%.
1959	Eisenhower (R)	Dow +16.4%, S&P +8.5%.
1963	Kennedy/Johnson (D)	Dow +17.0%, S&P +18.9%.
1967	Johnson (D)	Dow +15.2%, S&P +20.1%.
1971	Nixon (R)	Dow +6.1%, S&P +10.8%, NASDAQ +27.4%.
1975	Ford (R)	Dow +38.3%, S&P +31.5%, NASDAQ +29.8%.
1979	Carter (D)	Dow +4.2%, S&P +12.3%, NASDAQ +28.1%.
1983	Reagan (R)	Dow +20.3%, S&P +17.3%, NASDAQ +19.9%.

Table 5.4   (*Continued*)

Year	President	Result
1987	Reagan (R)	Dow +2.3%, S&P +2.0% despite Oct. meltdown. NASDAQ −5.4%.
1991	G.H.W. Bush (R)	Dow +20.3%, S&P +26.3%, NASDAQ +56.8%.
1995	Clinton (D)	Dow +33.5%, S&P +34.1%, NASDAQ +39.9%.
1999	Clinton (D)	Millennial fever crescendo: Dow +25.2%, S&P +19.5%, NASDAQ +85.6%.
2003	G.W. Bush (R)	Straight up after fall of Saddam Hussein: Dow +25.3% S&P +26.4%, NASDAQ +50.0%.
2007	G.W. Bush (R)	Credit bubble fuels all-time market highs before bear starts & Great Recession: Dow: +6.4%, S&P: +3.5%, NASDAQ: 9.8%.
2011	Obama (D)	European debt crisis: Dow: +5.5% S&P: −0.003%, NASDAQ: −1.8%.

England's Sir Winston Churchill, lost power in July 1945 shortly after the Allies' overwhelming defeat of the enemy.) In the modern era only Truman, in 1948, managed to retain power for the Democrats after WWII was over when he ran against a candidate (Dewey), who was heavily favored to win. With Iraq and the war on terror still in progress during 2004, Bush's popularity was still strong. Stocks did not run away during these six election years.

Voters usually "rally round the flag" when wars are in progress or threatening. During the twentieth century, elected presidents successfully running for second terms included Wilson (1916) prior to World War 1 and Roosevelt (1940) for a third term prior to the United States being involved in the Second World War. Roosevelt was elected again (1944) for a fourth term and Nixon (1972) won his second term, as wars were in progress. The Dow declined in the first two instances and climbed in the latter two. In the previous century, Madison was reelected during the War of 1812 and Lincoln (1864) in the midst of the Civil War.

Excepting exogenous events, markets tend to do better when incumbent presidents are reelected, rather than ousted. If you tally up the 13 occasions in the last 100 years when elected presidents ran for reelection, you get an average gain of 6.9 percent on the Dow when incumbents are reelected, compared to 0.9 percent on average when they lose. Of the nine winners, the five running during wars (or when there was a threat of war) saw average gains on the Dow of 2.6 percent. Gains for the four others, Roosevelt, Eisenhower, Reagan, and Clinton, averaged 12.4 percent.

Power in Washington changed hands 10 times since 1900. For most of the century Democrats gave up the White House after foreign entanglements were over or turned sour, while Republicans had to move out after things went awry on our own shores. In addition to the wars listed above Democrats were ousted in 1980 during the Iran hostage crisis. Republicans lost it domestically in 1912 (party split), 1932 (depression), 1960 (recession), 1976 (Watergate), and 2008 (financial crisis).

Dow Gains 9 Percent When Sitting President Runs

Since the inception of the Dow Jones Industrial Average in 1896 there have been 19 presidential elections in which a sitting president was running for reelection. DJIA posted gains in 14 of these 19 election years. There were only two losses greater than 5 percent. In 1932 as the Great Depression took hold, the DJIA fell 23.1 percent and President Hoover lost his reelection bid during the worst bear market in the Dow's history that brought the blue chip average down 86 percent from April 1930 to July 1932. He was also the only incumbent to lose the office when the market was down.

Ironically, the DJIA posted gains during the four other election years when the incumbent lost. As WWII ravaged Europe in 1940, DJIA lost 12.7 percent. In all 19 years the DJIA gained 9 percent on average. When the incumbent was reelected DJIA gained 10.7 percent versus 4.3 percent in the years the incumbent was ousted. Markets feed off of a popular president or rally in celebration after an unpopular president is replaced. You can see this in Table 5.5.

Table 5.5   Election Year DJIA % Change Since 1896—What Happens When the Sitting President Runs for Reelection

Year	President	DJIA %		
1900	McKinley (R)	7.0	Won	
1904	T. Roosevelt (R)	41.7	Won	T. Roosevelt took office after McKinley death.
1912	Taft (R)	7.6	Lost	
1916	Wilson (D)	−4.2	Won	
1924	Coolidge (R)	26.2	Won	Coolidge took office after Harding death.
1932	Hoover (R)	−23.1	Lost	
1936	F. Roosevelt (D)	24.8	Won	
1940	F. Roosevelt (D)	−12.7	Won	
1944	F. Roosevelt (D)	12.1	Won	
1948	Truman (D)	−2.1	Won	Truman took office after FDR death.
1956	Eisenhower (R)	2.3	Won	
1964	Johnson (D)	14.6	Won	Johnson took office after Kennedy death.
1972	Nixon (R)	14.6	Won	
1976	Ford (R)	17.9	Lost	Ford took office after Nixon resigned.
1980	Carter (D)	14.9	Lost	
1984	Reagan (R)	−3.7	Won	
1992	G. H. W. Bush (R)	4.2	Lost	
1996	Clinton (D)	26.0	Won	
2004	G. W. Bush (R)	3.1	Won	
	Average % Gain	**9.0%**		
	# Up/# Down		**14/5**	
	Wins	**10.7%**		
	Losses	**4.3%**		

Only Two Losses Last Seven Months of Election Years

Election years are traditionally up years. Incumbent administrations shamelessly attempt to massage the economy so voters will keep them in power. But, sometimes overpowering events occur and the market crumbles, usually resulting in a change of political control. The Republicans won in 1920 as the postwar economy contracted and President Wilson ailed. The Democrats came back during the 1932 Depression when the Dow hit its lowest level of the twentieth century. A world at war and the fall of France jolted the market in 1940 but Roosevelt won an unprecedented third term. Cold War confrontations and Truman's historic upset of Dewey held markets down through the end of 1948.

Since 1948, investors have barely been bruised during election years, except for a brief span early in the year—until 2000 and then again in 2008. In both years a bubble burst: technology and Internet stocks in 2000 and credit in 2008. Barring another massive regulatory failure, financial crisis, political miscalculation, or exogenous event, this is unlikely to occur again in 2012.

The last seven or eight months of election years are generally very positive, considering:

- Since 1952, January through April losses occurred in 8 of 15 election years. Incumbent parties were ousted on six of these eight losses. Ironically, bear markets commenced following four of seven gainers in 1956, 1968, 1973, and 1976.

- Comparing month-end June with month-end April reveals gains in 1952, 1960, 1968, 1988, and 2000 for the 60-day period when no sitting president ran for reelection.

- Of the 15 Julys since 1952, 9 were losers (1960, 1968, 1976, 1984, 1988, 1996, 2000, 2004, and 2008). Five were years when, at convention time, no strong incumbent was running for reelection. Note that April through July periods had six losers, the last four in a row: 1972 by a small margin, 1984 as the market was turning around, 1996 and 2000 as the bubble began to work off its excesses, 2004 and 2008 as the credit bubble burst.

- For a longer perspective, we extended the table to December. Just three losing eight-month periods in an election year are revealed and only two losses in the last seven months of all these years.

Incumbent Victories versus Incumbent Defeats

Since 1944, stocks have tended to move up earlier when White House occupants are popular but do even better in November and December when unpopular administrations are ousted (see Figure 5.3).

Figure 5.3   Trend of S&P 500 Index in Election Years 1944–2008

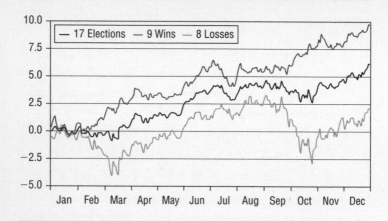

March, June, October, and December are best when incumbents stay in power, while July is worst. January, February, September, and October are the worst when they are removed. Ironically, November is best when incumbents are ousted and second worst when they win.

Other interesting tidbits: There were no major losses in October (1984 off fractionally) and only one in June and December when incumbent parties retained the White House. Republican wins in November resulted in total gains of 23.6 percent (excluding no-decision 2000). Democratic victories produced total losses of 4.9 percent in November; however, Democrats "gained" 16.4 percent in December, the Republicans 7.9 percent.

At a Glance

- Politics and elections have a clear impact on markets. Wars and unpopular policies usually occur in the first or second year of a presidential term, frequently triggering bear markets. From the post-election year high to the midterm low, the Dow has lost 20.9 percent on average since 1913.
- But by the third year, preelection year, the administration's focus shifts to "priming the pump." Policies are enacted to improve the economic well-being of the country and its electorate. From the midterm low to the preelection year high, the Dow has gained nearly 50 percent on average since 1914.

Chapter Six

Open Season for Stocks

*When to Trade Seasonal Trends
for Reliable Returns*

THERE IS NO SUCH thing as a perfect trading strategy, tactic, or methodology, but our Best Six Months Switching has an undeniable track record. The Best Six Months are basically the flipside of the old "sell in May and go away" adage. Market seasonality is a reflection of cultural behavior. In the old days, farming was the big driver, making August the best market month—now it's one of the worst.

This matches the summer vacation behavior where traders and investors prefer the golf course, beach, or poolside to the trading floor or computer screen. Institutions' efforts to beef up their numbers help drive the market higher in the fourth quarter as does holiday shopping and an influx of year-end bonus money.

Then there's the New Year, which tends to bring a positive new-leaf mentality to forecasts and predictions and the anticipation of strong fourth- and first-quarter earnings. After that, trading volume tends to decline throughout the summer and then in September there's back-to-school, back-to-work, and end-of-third-quarter portfolio window dressing that has caused stocks to sell off in September, making it the worst month of the year on average. Though we may be experiencing some shifts in seasonality, the record still shows the clear existence of seasonal trends in the stock market.

The "Best Six Months" Trading Strategy

Our Best Six Months Switching Trading Strategy consistently delivers. Investing in the Dow Jones Industrial Average between November 1st and April 30th each year and then switching into fixed income for the other six months has produced reliable returns with reduced risk since 1950.

November, December, January, March, and April are the top months since 1950. Add in February, and you have an impressive trading strategy. These six consecutive months gained 14,654.27 Dow points in 62 years, up 37 times and down 25, while the remaining May through October months lost 1,654.97 points, up 48 and down 14. The S&P gained 1,477.55 points in the same best six months versus a loss of 97.71 points in the worst six.

Figure 6.1 shows percentage changes for the Dow along with a compounding $10,000 investment. The

Figure 6.1   Six-Month Switching Strategy 1950–2012

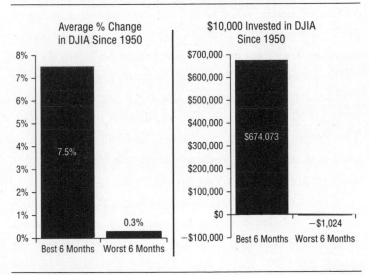

November to April $674,073 gain overshadows May to October's $1,024 loss. Just three November to April losses were double-digit: April 1970 (Cambodian invasion), 1973 (OPEC oil embargo), and 2008 (financial crisis). Similarly, Iraq muted the Best Six and inflated the Worst Six in 2003. When we discovered this strategy in 1986, November to April outperformed May to October by $88,163 to minus $1,522. Results improved substantially these past 25 years, $585,910 to $498.

Times They Are a Changing

The changing seasonal landscape has lengthened the favorable season, and I have been making adjustments to get in and out of the Best Six Months at more opportune times, either earlier or later, as market conditions dictate. I will explain how to do that in the final chapter. After the first back-to-back decline in the Best Six Months since 1974, in 2007 to 2009 the Worst Months soared in 2009. This is precisely what transpired back at the bottom in 1974 and the strategy exceled during the sideways market years of the late 1970s and early 1980s.

NASDAQ's amazing eight-month run from November through June illustrates that the times they are a changing. A $10,000 investment in these eight months since 1971 gained $384,337 (as of May 31, 2012) versus a loss of $3,196 during the void that is the four-month period July to October.

Seasonal trading strategies using the NASDAQ, Dow, and S&P averages for different monthly periods are displayed in Table 6.1. Most outstanding is the eight-month period for NASDAQ. In all the Best Months periods NASDAQ trounces the S&P about two or more to one.

Fourth-Quarter Market Magic

Examining market performance on a quarterly basis reveals several intriguing and helpful patterns. Fourth-quarter market gains have been magical, providing the greatest and most consistent gains over the years. First-quarter performance runs a respectable second. This should not be surprising as cash inflows, trading volume, and buying bias are generally elevated during these two quarters.

Positive market psychology hits a fever pitch as the holiday season approaches and does not begin to wane until spring. Professionals drive the market higher as they make portfolio adjustments to maximize year-end numbers. Bonuses are paid and invested around the turn of the year.

The market's sweet spot of the Four-Year Cycle begins in the fourth quarter of the midterm year. The best two-quarter span runs from the fourth quarter of the midterm year through the first quarter of the preelection year, averaging 15.3 percent for the Dow, 16.0 percent for the S&P 500 and an amazing 23.3 percent for NASDAQ.

Quarterly strength fades in the latter half of the preelection year, but stays impressively positive through

Table 6.1 $10,000 Invested in NASDAQ, S&P, & Dow Best vs. Worst Months since 1971

Months	Best Months	NASDAQ	S&P	Dow	Months	Worst Months	NASDAQ	S&P	Dow
9	Oct 1–Jun 30	$350,180	$167,390	$175,769	3	Jul 1–Sep 30	–$ 3,795	–$ 3,624	–$ 3,433
8	Nov 1–Jun 30	$356,169	$144,829	$170,089	4	Jul 1–Oct 31	–$ 3,197	–$ 1,906	–$ 2,539
8	Oct 1–May 31	$273,992	$153,668	$187,038	4	Jun 1–Sep 30	–$ 2,133	–$ 3,054	–$ 3,892
6	Nov 1–Apr 30	$192,319	$ 97,502	$152,245	6	May 1–Oct 31	$ 1,838	$ 1,221	–$ 2,228
4	Nov 1–Feb 28	$ 99,775	$ 34,369	$ 40,846	8	Mar 1–Oct 31	$16,603	$21,866	$19,019
3	Nov 1–Jan 31	$ 91,774	$ 36,991	$ 38,963	9	Feb 1–Oct 31	$17,997	$19,288	$19,681

the election year. Losses dominate the first and third quarter of post-election years and the first and second quarters of midterm years. Take a look at Table 6.2.

Two Market Phenomena in Perfect Harmony

In a continuing effort to improve, prove, and debunk market axioms, patterns, and strategies, I combined two of the most pervasive market phenomena: the Best Six Months and the Four-Year Cycle. Though they are not perfect, these two trends have stood the test of time.

Recurring seasonal stock market patterns and the Four-Year Presidential Election/Stock Market Cycle have been integral to our research since the first *Almanac* 46 years ago. Yale Hirsch discovered the Best Six Months in 1986, and it has been a cornerstone of our seasonal investment analysis and strategies ever since.

Most of the market's gains have occurred during the Best Six Months, and the market generally hits a low point every four years in the first (post-election) or second (midterm) year and exhibits the greatest gains in the third (preelection) year. As the market wrestles with midterm year machinations and the summer comes to a close we hit the sweet spot of the Four-Year Cycle.

You can combine the best of these two market phenomena and only need to make four trades every four years to nearly triple the results of the Best Six Months. As depicted in Table 6.3, using a simple timing indicator

Table 6.2 Quarterly Percent Changes for the Dow, S&P, and NASDAQ

	Q1	Q2	Q3	Q4	Year	Q2–Q3	Q4–Q1
Dow Jones Industrials (1949–March 2012)							
Average	2.1%	1.6%	0.4%	3.9%	8.2%	2.0%	6.3%
Post-Election	−1.1%	1.6%	0.2%	3.4%	4.4%	1.8%	5.2%
Midterm	1.5%	−1.8%	−0.5%	7.3%	6.7%	−2.2%	**15.3%**
Preelection	7.5%	5.3%	1.6%	2.3%	17.7%	6.8%	3.2%
Election	0.8%	1.2%	0.4%	2.3%	4.6%	1.6%	1.2%
S&P 500 (1949–March 2012)							
Average	2.0%	1.7%	0.5%	4.1%	8.6%	2.3%	6.6%
Post-Election	−1.2%	2.2%	0.4%	3.1%	4.8%	2.7%	4.3%
Midterm	1.0%	−2.8%	0.1%	8.0%	6.4%	−2.7%	**16.0%**
Preelection	7.5%	5.2%	1.1%	3.0%	17.1%	6.3%	4.6%
Election	1.4%	2.1%	0.6%	2.1%	6.1%	2.6%	1.0%
NASDAQ Composite (1971–March 2012)							
Average	4.4%	3.3%	−0.4%	4.4%	11.9%	3.2%	9.1%
Post-Election	−3.3%	6.8%	1.3%	4.2%	8.4%	8.1%	6.3%
Midterm	2.1%	−3.4%	−5.2%	8.9%	1.7%	−8.1%	**23.3%**
Preelection	13.8%	8.0%	1.7%	5.1%	30.9%	12.1%	7.8%
Election	3.9%	1.3%	0.6%	−0.6%	4.8%	2.4%	−3.1%

Table 6.3   Four Trades Every Four Years

Year	Worst Six Months: May–October	Best Six Months: November–April
Post-Election	Sell	Buy
Midterm	Sell	Buy
Preelection	Hold	Hold
Election	Hold	Hold

discussed in the final chapter of this book you can buy and sell during the post-election and midterm years and then hold from October 1 in the midterm year until the post-election year sometime after April 1, approximately 2.5 years. Better returns, less effort, lower transaction fees, and fewer taxable events.

Seasonally Well Adjusted

Stocks may fluctuate as J.P. Morgan said, but they usually do so in the same pattern every year. Although technology and human habits are continually changing and shifting, the market repeats the same cycle year after year. In a typical year, the bulk of the market's gains occur in just six months, November through April. By investing in the market during just these months, risk is cut in half (or better as many significant declines have taken place from May to October), gains are more consistent, and summer can be more enjoyable.

But the Best Six Months are not only to be used as a trading tactic or investing strategy. Use your knowledge

of seasonal market patterns to make better overall investment decisions. If the market has just made a big move up
from October to March, it's a good idea not to get so
aggressive and pour a lot of money into the stock market.
On the other hand if the market has declined significantly
and then turns around strongly in October that's likely a
better time to take long-term positions.

Finally, seasonal patterns can be an indicator in and
of themselves. The market's decline from October 2007
to March 2008 was a clear warning sign that stocks were
ripe for a fall. The Dow's 50 percent gain from March to
September 2009 was a solid sign that the global financial
crisis, the Great Recession, and worst bear market in a
generation was over.

At a Glance

- The Best Six Months of the year are November
  through April.
- A simple trading strategy of switching into stocks
  during October and November and out of
  stocks in April and May increases profits in most
  years and reduces risk.
- Paying attention to seasonal stock market patterns provides insight to the market and aide in
  all investment decisions.

Chapter Seven

Aura of the Witch

~

*Timing Your Trades around
Options Expiration Dates*

SINCE THE EARLY DAYS of the *Stock Trader's Almanac* back
in the late 1960s, we knew options expiration had a profound impact on the stock market. We have been remind-
ing investors of the expiration of stock options ever since.
Initially, it was just a written notation on the annual strategy calendars. Then, in 1977, we added a circle around
the expiration dates so users could see them at a glance. In
1987, a skull and crossbones icon was placed in the weekly

calendar pages on the third Friday of each month to alert folks to the increased volatility around options expiration.

One year later in the 1988 edition we put three skull and crossbones icons on the third Friday of March, June, September, and December when stock index futures contracts expired, embracing the new term "Triple Witching" that had become popular on Wall Street. In 2001, we replaced the skull and crossbones with the witch icon we currently use today. Just as the moon affects the tide the expiration of options and futures contracts pulls the stock market into a cycle of volatility that flows cash into and out of the market, which drives the direction of stock prices.

Financial Incantations

Traders have long sought to understand and master the magic of this quarterly phenomenon. On the third Friday of every month options expire but in March, June, September, and December a powerful coven gathers. Since the S&P index futures began trading in June 1982 stock options, index options, as well as index futures all expire at the same time four times each year—known as Triple Witching.

With the recent advent of single-stock futures some have used the term "quadruple witching." But the market is still relatively small for single-stock futures so the name has not fully caught on. Even the recent proliferation of weekly and other nonstandard option contracts has not been able to diminish the influence of equity index futures or dethrone the cycle of Triple Witching.

Increased volatility and trading volume across the equity exchanges is often associated with Triple Witching— the Friday of expiration and the days leading up to it. An examination of Triple-Witching patterns and seasonalities casts a ray of light on these mystical conjurations and helps you summon an edge and hopefully increase profits while warding off losses.

For years we have analyzed what the market does prior to, during, and following Triple-Witching expirations in search of consistent trading patterns. This is never easy, for as soon as a pattern becomes obvious, the market almost always tends to anticipate it and the pattern tends to shift. These are some of our findings of how the Dow Jones Industrials perform around Triple-Witching time.

Seasons of the Witch

Triple-Witching Weeks have become more bullish in the last decade. The weeks following Triple-Witching Weeks have become more bearish, especially in the second quarter. There has not been a positive week after June Triple-Witching Week since 1998. Triple-Witching Weeks have tended to be down in flat periods and dramatically so during bear markets.

Down weeks tend to follow down Triple-Witching Weeks. This is a most interesting pattern. Since 1991, of 29 down Triple-Witching Weeks, 21 following weeks were also down. This is surprising inasmuch as the previous decade had an exactly opposite pattern: there were 13 down Triple-Witching Weeks then, but 12 up weeks followed them.

When we break down Triple-Witching Weeks quarter by quarter an even clearer pattern emerges. You can clearly see in Table 7.1 that Triple-Witching Weeks in the second and third quarter are much weaker and the weeks following, horrendous. But in the first and fourth quarter a solid bullish bias is evident.

It's not coincidental that these strong Triple-Witching Weeks occur during the Best Six Months period November through April while trading around Triple-Witching Weeks is rather dismal in the Worst Six Months May through October.

Since 1991, second-quarter Triple-Witching Weeks have been up 12 times and down 9. Following weeks were atrocious, down 19 and up only 2 times. One up week followed the 6 up Triple-Witching Weeks whereas 8 down weeks followed 9 down Triple-Witching Weeks.

Third-quarter Triple-Witching Weeks were slightly better, up 13 of the last 21 times. But weeks following Triple Witching were down 16 of the last 21. Four up

Table 7.1 Triple-Witching Week and Week after Dow Point Changes

	Expiration Week Q1	Week After	Expiration Week Q2	Week After	Expiration Week Q3	Week After	Expiration Week Q4	Week After
1991	−6.93	−89.36	−34.98	−58.81	33.54	−13.19	20.12	167.04
1992	40.48	−44.95	−69.01	−2.94	21.35	−76.73	9.19	12.97
1993	43.76	−31.60	−10.24	−3.88	−8.38	−70.14	10.90	6.15
1994	32.95	−120.92	3.33	−139.84	58.54	−101.60	116.08	26.24
1995	38.04	65.02	86.80	75.05	96.85	−33.42	19.87	−78.76
1996	114.52	51.67	55.78	−50.60	49.94	−15.54	179.53	76.51
1997	−130.67	−64.20	14.47	−108.79	174.30	4.91	−82.01	−76.98
1998	303.91	−110.35	−122.07	231.67	100.16	133.11	81.87	314.36
1999	27.20	−81.31	365.05	−303.00	−224.80	−524.30	32.73	148.33
2000	666.41	517.49	−164.76	−44.55	−293.65	−79.63	−277.95	200.60
2001	−821.21	−318.63	−353.36	−19.05	−1369.70	611.75	224.19	101.65
2002	34.74	−179.56	−220.42	−10.53	−326.67	−284.57	77.61	−207.54
2003	662.26	−376.20	83.63	−211.70	173.27	−331.74	236.06	46.45
2004	−53.48	26.37	6.31	−44.57	−28.61	−237.22	106.70	177.20
2005	−144.69	−186.80	110.44	−325.23	−36.62	−222.35	97.01	7.68

(Continued)

Table 7.1 (Continued)

	Expiration Week Q1	Week After	Expiration Week Q2	Week After	Expiration Week Q3	Week After	Expiration Week Q4	Week After
2006	203.31	0.32	122.63	−25.46	168.66	−52.67	138.03	−102.30
2007	−165.91	370.60	215.09	−279.22	377.67	75.44	110.80	−84.78
2008	410.23	−144.92	−464.66	−496.18	−33.55	−245.31	−50.57	−63.56
2009	54.40	497.80	−259.53	−101.34	214.79	−155.01	−142.61	191.21
2010	117.29	108.38	239.57	−306.83	145.08	252.41	81.59	81.58
2011	−185.88	362.07	52.45	−69.78	516.96	−737.61	−317.87	427.61
2012	310.60	−151.89						
Up	15	9	12	2	13	5	16	15
Down	7	13	9	19	8	16	5	6

[110]

weeks followed the 13 up Triple-Witching Weeks and 7 down weeks followed the 8 down Triple-Witching Weeks.

The tables turn dramatically in the first and fourth quarters. First-quarter Triple-Witching Weeks perform quite well up 15 of the last 22 but weeks following have been down 13 times. Six up weeks followed the 15 up Triple-Witching Weeks and 4 down weeks followed the 7 down Triple-Witching Weeks.

Fourth-quarter Triple Witching has proved to be the most favorable. Triple-Witching Week was up 16 of the last 21 times and the following week was up 15 of 21 times. Twelve up weeks followed the 16 up Triple-Witching Weeks and 2 down weeks followed the 5 down Triple-Witching Weeks.

Manic Monday and Freaky Friday

I place a considerable degree of importance on the market's performance on Mondays and Fridays. How traders behave at the beginnings and ends of weeks can be indicative of the market's future course. Therefore, market performance on the Monday before Triple Witching and on expiration Friday possesses even greater significance.

March Triple-Witching Monday has been up 15 of the last 22 while Friday is up only 11 of those times. In June, Monday is up 11 of 21 and Friday has risen 12 times. In September, now the worst month of the year, Monday before Triple Witch is up 14 of the last 21 occurrences and Friday 13 times (8 straight 2004–2011). December, one of the year's top months, has experienced the most bullishness at Triple Witching time in recent years. On Mondays of December Triple Witching the Dow has advanced 12 of the past 21 years and Fridays saw gains in 13 of those years.

This further underscores the trepidations traders and investors face during the often-volatile month of March. Being positioned ahead of the normally bullish March Triple-Witching Week, while using strength that week to lock in some gains, may be the wisest course for those investing for shorter time frames. Short-term tops often occur during March Triple-Witching Week.

Witches' Brew

As I learned the business and became intimate with the seasonal tendencies of the stock market, the cycle of expiration Friday and Triple Witching was clear. A financial transaction event that occurs with such consistent regularity and involves the transfer of massive amounts of money by the largest financial institutions around the world has created one of the most discernible cyclical patterns in the stock market.

It is crucial to be mindful of these quarterly affairs when you make adjustments to your portfolio. For the most part you will be better served adding long positions

the week after Triple Witching and taking profits during
Triple-Witching Week. And remember that both the week
of and after Triple Witching are especially volatile during
June and September with a distinctly negative bias.

At a Glance

- Quarterly stock options, stock index options,
  and stock index futures expiration in March,
  June, September, and December—"Triple
  Witching"—has a deep impact on the market,
  creating distinct patterns.
- Expiration week is strongest during the Best Six
  Months of the year in December and March, less
  bullish during June and September.
- The week after is best avoided in all but December.
  And just because there is a healthy gain in expiration week, don't expect further gains in the week
  after. Down weeks however, do have a habit of
  following down weeks.

Chapter Eight

Autumn Planting

~

When the Seeds of Most Market Gains Are Planted

HUMAN NATURE SYNCHRONIZES MARKET seasonality with Mother Nature to a degree. But market gains are predominantly sown in the late summer and early fall and reaped in winter and spring. Monthly seasonal patterns are arranged in the next four chapters in a different array than they are on the calendar in line with seasonal movements of the stock market.

I begin discussing monthly seasonal tendencies with August because quite simply, 11 of the last 19 bear market bottoms (in the modern era since 1950) have fallen in August, September, or October. More recently, since 1982, six of the last eight have ended in these months. These are the best months to establish new long positions or add money to existing holdings when prices are frequently much more attractive.

August Annals

In the first half of the twentieth century, money flow from harvesting made August a great stock market month. In fact, it was the best month from 1901 to 1951. In 1900, 37.5 percent of the population was farming. Now less than 2 percent farm, and August is one of the worst months of the year. August has become the worst S&P 500 month in the past 15 years.

The shortest bear market in history (45 days) caused by turmoil in Russia, the Asian currency crisis, and the Long-Term Capital Management hedge fund debacle ended August 31, 1998. The Dow dropped a record 1,344.22 points for the month, off 15.1 percent—which is the second worst monthly percentage Dow loss since 1950. The Dow lost 512.61 points on the day, –6.4 percent, which at the time was the worst one-day drop since October 1987. Saddam Hussein triggered a 10.0 percent slide in August

1990. The best Dow gains occurred in 1982 (11.5 percent) and 1984 (9.8 percent) as bear markets ended.

Trading stocks in August has led to frustration with its propensity for nasty sell-offs. August's woes may be perpetuated by the empty trading floors of the popular vacation month.

August is its typical self in post-election years generating losses and ranking last on the Dow Jones Industrials. It is the penultimate S&P 500, NASDAQ, and Russell 1000 month and third from the bottom for the Russell 2000. Midterm Augusts behave on par with the month's overall weak performance. Preelection Augusts produce decent gains and rank a bit higher on the Dow Industrials and S&P 500. Election year Augusts perform better though; ranked number one on both Russell indices with the small cap Russell 2000 averaging a 3.5 percent gain, up 5, down 3.

On Monday of expiration the Dow has been up 15 of the last 22 times with some big winners while on expiration Friday it has dropped in 12 of those years. Expiration week as a whole is down more than half the time with some steep losses. In 2011, the Dow shed 4 percent in the week. The week after is modestly stronger. After being up five straight years from 2000 to 2004, it has been down four of the last seven. A 4.3-percent rally in 2011 erased all of the previous week's losses.

The first nine trading days of the month have exhibited weakness while mid-month is strongest. The end of August tends to get whacked as traders evacuate Wall Street for the summer finale. The last 5 days have suffered in 10 of the last 16 years with the Dow up only 4 times the next-to-last day in the past 16 years. Over the same time period, the last five days of August have averaged losses of: Dow Jones Industrials, –1.5 percent; S&P 500, –1.3 percent; and NASDAQ, –1.0 percent. Small caps have fared slightly better with Russell 2000 off just –0.2 percent.

September Scenarios

September has the dubious honor of being the worst month of the year and was creamed four years straight from 1999 to 2002 after four banner years from 1996 to 1998 in the halcyon days of the dot-com bubble madness. Though the month tends to open strong, once the summer tans begin to fade and the kids head back to school, fund managers tend to clean house as the end of the third quarter approaches, causing some nasty sell-offs near month-end over the years. I steer clear of the long side until the institutions settle up their accounts.

Post-election Septembers, though not the worst post-election year month, are prone to large declines. Nine of the last 15 post-election year Septembers took some rather mean hits. Six gains came with great cause. The 1953 bear market ended in September. An acceleration of defense spending in September 1965 related to Vietnam created a bullish environment for stocks. The 1973 downleg ended in August, though the Yom Kippur War, Watergate, and the OPEC oil embargo forged a wicked bear market through 1973 and 1974. President Clinton's signing of the capital gains tax cut into law in July 1997 helped boost stocks in September 1997; August and October were down 7.3 percent and 6.3 percent, respectively. In 2005, after Hurricane Katrina ravaged New Orleans the market rebounded in September. Historic fiscal and monetary stimulus, in response to the global financial crisis, sent markets nearly straight up from July 2009 to April 2010.

Midterm Septembers have punished investors ahead of eight October midterm bottoms since WWII. Along with October, September is the other weak link in mighty preelection years. Just 4 S&P 500 losses came in the last 11 election year Septembers—in 1972 and 1984 when incumbents ran and won; in 2000, down over 5 percent, during the incumbent-less "fuzzy" campaigns; and in 2008 as Lehman Brothers fell into bankruptcy.

Except for the Monday before, September Triple Witching is not to be trifled with. The Dow has risen 15 of the last 22 years on Monday. Triple-Witching Friday has been up eight straight years from 2004 through 2011, but the longer term record is much less bullish with just 13 advances in the past 22 years. Triple-Witching Week can be cruel, especially in bear markets. The week after Triple Witching has been brutal, down 17 of the last 22, averaging a Dow loss of 1.2 percent.

Despite its bad reputation, September has a few bullish tendencies. Its 11th trading day is the month's silver lining, with the Dow Jones Industrials posting gains in 8 of the last 10 years. Gains have averaged 0.6 percent, while the Dow has accumulated an amazing 720.24 points on this day. As mentioned, the Monday before Triple Witching exhibits a consistent record of strength. Other than those few days an abundance of hazards shrouds the month, especially the second half. The third to last trading is the best of the last two weeks with the Dow up 8 of the past 10 years. The last day of the month has been down in 8 of the past 10 years.

In every instance that the DJIA was positive for September in the midterm year, the low was already in place and a fresh leg of a rally was under way. In Table 8.1 midterm years are ranked in descending order of September gains for the Dow, accompanied by the percent

Table 8.1 Big Midterm Septembers since 1901 Came after Low

Year	Midterm Low Date	Midterm Low DJIA	Sept % Gain	Oct % Gain	Nov % Gain	Dec % Gain	Year % Gain	Preelection High Date	Preelection High DJIA	Rally
2010	Jul 02	9686.48	7.7	3.1	−1.0	5.2	11.0	Apr 29	12810.54	32.3%
1954	Jan 11	279.87	7.3	−2.3	9.8	4.6	44.0	Dec 30	488.40	74.5
1958	Feb 25	436.89	4.6	2.1	2.6	4.7	34.0	Dec 31	679.36	55.5
1950	Jan 13	196.81	4.4	−0.6	1.2	3.4	17.6	Sep 13	276.37	40.4
1998	Aug 31	7539.07	4.0	9.6	6.1	0.7	16.1	Dec 31	11497.12	52.5
1942	Apr 28	92.92	2.6	4.5	0.4	4.3	7.6	Jul 14	145.82	56.9
2006	Jan 20	10667.39	2.6	3.4	1.2	2.0	16.3	Oct 09	14164.53	32.8
1918	Jan 15	73.38	2.2	1.0	−5.1	1.3	10.5	Nov 03	119.62	63.0
1938	Mar 31	98.95	1.6	7.3	−1.3	3.3	28.1	Sep 12	155.92	57.6
1906	Jul 13	62.40	0.9	−2.0	2.4	−0.8	−1.9	Jan 07	70.60	13.1
1910	Jul 26	53.93	0.1	6.3	−2.7	−1.4	−17.9	Jun 19	63.78	18.3
1914	Jul 30	52.32	World War I			4.3	−5.4	Dec 27	99.21	89.6
	Average		3.5	2.9	1.2	2.5	15.0			48.9%

changes for the remaining months of the year, the year's change, and the midterm-low-to-preelection-high rally.

October Occasions

October often evokes fear on Wall Street as memories are stirred of crashes in 1929, 1987, the 554-point drop on October 27, 1997, back-to-back massacres in 1978 and 1979, Friday the 13th in 1989, and the 733-point drop on October 15, 2008. The term "Octoberphobia" has been used to describe the phenomenon of major market drops occurring during the month. Market calamities can become a self-fulfilling prophecy, so stay on the lookout and don't get whipsawed if it happens.

But it has become a turnaround month—a "bear killer," if you will. Twelve post-World War II bear markets have ended in October: 1946, 1957, 1960, 1962, 1966, 1974, 1987, 1990, 1998, 2001, 2002, and 2011. Eight were midterm bottoms.

Twice during the four decades of newsletter publishing we have jumped on these major midterm October bottoms and advised subscribers likewise with bold headlines of "BUY! BUY! BUY! BUY! BUY! BUY! BUY! BUY! BUY! BUY!" across the top. In October 1974, Yale Hirsch had the guts to go out on a limb in the face of Watergate, the OPEC Oil Embargo, and the worst bear market since the Great Depression. And most recently in 2002, we repeated the coup de grace on October 16, days after the end of the bear market that brought NASDAQ down 77.9 percent from its year 2000 top as the worst bear market since the 1970s gnashed its teeth with rampant corporate malfeasance, terrorism, memories of 9/11, Afghanistan, and the looming confrontation with Iraq.

October used to be a horrible month for stocks and from 1950 to 1997 held the record for most cumulative Dow Jones Industrials points lost. Since the beating in 1997 it has been the second best month, up 11 of the last 14 years. October 2011 was only the second month in which the Dow gained more than 1,000 points. April 1999 was the first. The "Worst Months" of the year ends with October. With October a rising market star and a frequent bear killer it has become one of the best times of the year to take long positions.

October does fairly well in post-election years as other months take the brunt of bearish crosscurrents. Midterm election year Octobers are downright stellar thanks to the major turnarounds mentioned previously; ranking number one on the Dow, S&P 500, NASDAQ, and Russell 1000; and second on the Russell 2000. October has been the weakest link in preelection years but has produced hefty gains in bull markets, most recently in 1999, 2003, and 2011. Octobers used to average about the same in election years as they do in all years, but 2008's abysmal performance has sunk the average. Usually October rises and falls with the incumbent's prospect for reelection in election years.

Options expiration week in October provides plenty of opportunity. On the Monday before expiration the Dow has only been down five times since 1982 and the Russell 2000 was up 17 years straight from 1990 to 2006, but it has been down 4 of the last 5. Expiration day has a more spotty record as does the week as a whole. After a market bottom in October, the week after is most bullish, otherwise it is susceptible to downdrafts. Any weakness can be used to take new long positions.

After mild gains the first couple of days, stocks tend to drift lower. Midmonth trading is more robust around options expiration. Weakness then plagues the third week of the month. Strength during the last several days is most dependable the second to last day with the Dow Industrials and S&P 500 up 14 of the past 21 years, averaging one-day gains between 0.5 and 0.7 percent.

Sowing the Seeds of Gains

A perfect storm of perennial circumstances fertilizes the ground for stocks from August to October. Reduced trading volume during the big vacation month of August removes a substantial number of buyers from the marketplace. Conventions and elections distract the country from buying stocks. Increased selling from end-of-third-portfolio maneuvers creates a vacuum that sucks down stock prices.

This is why so many bear market bottoms occur at this time of the year and why it is the best time to buy stocks.

At a Glance

- Best buying opportunities have come in August, September, or October over the past 62 years—the best three months to sow new long positions.
- The Worst Six Months of the year end in October, however, as seasonality shifts and front-runners anticipate, September and August have proven to be excellent times of the year to establish new long positions. October has become a bear killing turnaround month.
- October has posted the most bear market lows of any month.

Chapter Nine

Winter of Content

_~_

An Infusion of Cash and Good Tidings Blossoms into Healthy Market Gains

NOVEMBER, DECEMBER, AND JANUARY are the best three consecutive months of the year. Not only do the odds favor solid gains, the gains themselves can be staggering compared to all other months. If you were only to be invested for three months of any year, these are the months. Dow and S&P 500 have averaged a 4.3 percent gain since 1950 from November to January, while NASDAQ and the Russell 2000 rack up 6.4 percent.

Conversely, when this three-month span fails to deliver gains as it did in 2007 and 2008, it is a red-flag warning that is best heeded. The late market analyst Edson Gould said it best, "If the market does not rally, as it should during bullish seasonal periods, it is a sign that other forces are stronger and that when the seasonal period ends those forces will really have their say."

Navigating November

Ah, November, the holiday season begins and ushers in the start of the best months of the year. November ranks third or fourth depending on the time frame or index. It is the beginning of the Best Six Months for the Dow and S&P, and the Best Eight Months for NASDAQ. Small caps come into favor during November but they really take off the last two weeks of the year in December.

November maintains its status among the top-performing months as fourth-quarter cash inflows from institutions drive November to lead the best consecutive three-month span. The month has taken hits during bear markets. Tarnished by the undecided election and the nascent secular bear market, November 2000, down –22.9 percent, was NASDAQ's second worst month on record since the composite was created February 5, 1971—second only to October 1987.

November's market strength is apparent as it does not suffer from any consistent losses in any of the four years of the presidential election cycle. The Dow Jones Industrials lost ground in only three Novembers in the last 15 post-election years since 1953 (all during Vietnam); the S&P 500 was down only 4.

Midterm election Novembers team with October for a helluva one-two punch, an 8.1 percent two-month NASDAQ gain. Preelection year Novembers are ironically mediocre for such a powerful market year.

Election year Novembers rank number one for the Dow and S&P 500 but have relinquished losses in tumultuous election environments and the financial crisis of 2008. The year 2000 was the worst election year November since Truman upset Dewy in 1948 following the first undecided presidential election since 1888. Still reeling from the effects of Lehman Brother's bankruptcy in September 2008, markets tumbled a comparable amount in November 2008 as they did in November 2000.

Options expiration often coincides with the week before Thanksgiving. In any event the week is generally strong. Dow Jones Industrials posted 10 straight gains from 1993 to 2002, but has declined in 4 of the past 9 years. The Monday before expiration day has been streaky with the Dow up five straight years from 1994 to 1998, during the bulk of the last twentieth-century bull market, down five in a row, 1999 to 2003, and up five of the last eight. Options expiration day displays a similar pattern, though with a greater bullish bias, up 15 of the last 22. The week after expiration has taken it on the chin lately, down five of the last six years.

Being such a bullish month November is not surprisingly chockfull of strong days, though it does have weak points. Over the past 21 years the first and second trading days have been mixed with positive average daily gains for the Dow and S&P 500. NASDAQ and the Russell 2000 tend to start off stronger. The next three days have a bullish bias but the seventh trading day is characterized by market losses. After drifting sideways for several days stock prices tend to move higher just before midmonth, then fade for several days. At about five days before month-end, the market heats up as fourth-quarter rallies frequently take hold until the last day of the month when stocks pause before big December. The bond market closes for Veterans Day.

December Delivers

December is the number-two month on the Dow Jones Industrials and number one on the S&P 500 since 1950, averaging gains of 1.7 percent each. It's also the top-ranked month for small caps and second on NASDAQ. Rarely does the market fall precipitously in December.

When it does it is usually a turning point in the market—near a top or bottom. If the market has experienced fantastic gains leading up to December, stocks are likely ripe for a fall. Conversely, if the market has been through the wringer of late and December is down sharply as well, then expect a rally to ensue shortly. In 1998, December was part of best fourth quarter since 1928.

Market trading in December is holiday inspired and fueled by a buying bias throughout the month on the part of professional traders and brokerage houses. However, the first part of the month tends to be weaker as tax-loss selling and year-end portfolio restructuring crescendos. The month is laden with market seasonality and important events. As small caps tend to start to outperform larger caps near the middle of the month my "free lunch" strategy is served on Wall Street. Our "Santa Claus Rally" is the first indicator to register a reading in the New Year and begins the last week of December.

The S&P 500 has been down in only four Decembers the last 15 post-election years while the Dow was down 5. Only four Decembers lost ground in the last 16 midterm election years. The years 1966, 1974, and 2002 were major midterm bottoms; 2002 was the worst December since 1931, down over 6 percent on the Dow Industrials and S&P 500, and off 9.7 percent on NASDAQ. Since WWII the Dow Industrials have fallen only thrice in preelection year December: 1975 (–1.0 percent), 1983 (–1.4 percent), and 2007 (–0.8 percent). Election year Decembers fare well; the S&P 500 averages 1.2 percent, up 12 of the past 15.

December Triple-Witching Week is usually favorable to the Dow Jones Industrials with Monday up 12 of the last 22 years while Triple-Witching Friday is up 14 of those years. The entire week has logged gains an amazing 23 times since 1984. The week after December Triple Witching is the best of all weeks after and is the only one with a clearly bullish bias.

Since 1991, the first three trading days of the month have been strongest for NASDAQ and the Russell 2000. The Dow and S&P 500 start the month off slower and do not become undeniably bullish until the third trading day. But, on the fourth day trading becomes more guarded and remains so through the first half of the month as tax-loss selling wraps up. It is not until the middle of the week after December Triple-Witching Week that stocks begin to rise consistently on the majority of days.

The day before and after Christmas has been solid over the past 21 years with Dow gains 5 years straight on the day before and 4 of the past 6 days after. NASDAQ had a stellar record of being up the last trading day of the year 29 years in a row until 2000. Since then, NASDAQ has been down 11 times in 12 years. Less bullishness the last trading day of the year is due to last-minute portfolio restructuring.

I've taken the 34 years of daily data for the Russell 2000 index of smaller companies and divided it by the Russell 1000 index of largest companies. Then the data is compressed into a single year to show an idealized yearly pattern. When the graph in Figure 9.1 is descending, big blue chips are outperforming smaller companies; when the graph is rising, smaller companies are moving up faster than their larger brethren.

Figure 9.1   Russell 2000/Russell 1000 One-Year Seasonal Pattern

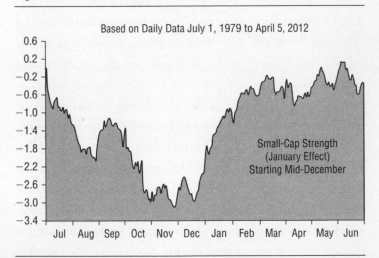

Figure 9.1 illustrates quite clearly that the "January effect" of small-cap stocks outperforming big-cap stocks in the month of January now starts in mid-December. Also noticeable are small stock moves in late October and late November. Any early December weakness in small stocks can be used to add to existing positions or make new ones. Note that the bulk of this move is complete by mid-January, but runs through early March. Any outsized gains can be taken without prejudice, especially by implementing my standard trading policy for small stocks of selling half on a double to take your initial investment off the table.

Wall Street's Only Free Lunch

The bottom-fishing strategy I have implemented over the years feeds off the year-end small-cap strength just discussed. My "free lunch" strategy is only an extremely short-term strategy reserved for the nimblest traders.

Tax-loss selling tends to push losing stocks down to bargain levels near year-end. In years past New York Stock Exchange stocks selling at their lows on December 15 usually outperformed the market by February 15 in the following year. Tax-loss selling usually climaxes around triple witching, so I make my selections from stocks making new 52-week lows on Triple-Witching Friday in order to capitalize on yearend strength.

The candidates are hand-picked. Preferred stocks, closed-end funds, exchange-traded funds, exchange-traded notes, splits, new issues, and nonregular common shares or sketchy outfits are eliminated. When there are a huge number of new lows, stocks down the most are selected.

The strategy was refined further when only a handful of NYSE stocks were left after my screens. Additional selections from NASDAQ and AMEX exchanges have demonstrated similar characteristics as NYSE stocks and have been added in recent years. These stocks tend to start giving back their gains in January, so I often sell in mid-January or when quick gains materialize.

The object is to buy bargain stocks near their 52-week lows and sell any quick, generous gains, as the stocks can often be real dogs. It's a quick trade, don't get attached to these stocks. When they pop, sell them. We're just trying to capitalize on any "dead cat bounce." If any of these stocks double, sell at least half, or use trailing stops so if they continue to rise you stay in, if not, you're out.

This free lunch strategy has performed better after market corrections and when there are more new lows at year-end. These annual bargain-stock baskets underperformed the NYSE Composite index in only 5 of the last 38 years. Average gains of 12.7 percent over the holding period handily beat the NYSE's 3.1 percent average by nearly 10 percentage points.

When Santa Fails to Call

Beginning just before or right after the market's Christmas closing, we normally experience a brief, yet respectable, rally from the last five trading days of the year through the first two of the New Year. The S&P 500 has averaged a 1.5 percent gain during this seven-day span since 1953. We refer to this as the "Santa Claus Rally."

It is more important when this reliable seasonality has failed to materialize. This has often been a harbinger of bear markets or sizeable corrections in the coming year. But these were times stocks could have been purchased later in the year at much lower prices. Yale Hirsch discovered this phenomenon in 1972. We have alerted investors to this ominous portent for decades with Yale's mnemonic device, "If Santa Claus should fail to call, bears may come to Broad and Wall."

Table 9.1 shows this rhyme was certainly on the mark in 2000, as the period suffered a horrendous 4.0 percent loss. On January 14, 2000, the Dow started its 33-month 37.8 percent slide to the October 2002 midterm election year bottom. NASDAQ cracked eight weeks later falling 37.3 percent in 10 weeks, eventually dropping 77.9 percent by October 2002.

Saddam Hussein's invasion of Kuwait cancelled 1990's Santa Claus Rally. Three days later, on January 9, 1991,

Table 9.1   Santa Claus Rally in the S&P 500

New Year	Rally %	Year %	
1953	1.8	−6.6	
1954	1.7	45.0	
1955	3.0	26.4	
1956	−0.9	2.6	April Top
1957	1.2	−14.3	
1958	3.5	38.1	
1959	3.6	8.5	
1960	2.4	−3.0	
1961	1.7	23.1	
1962	0.4	−11.8	
1963	1.7	18.9	
1964	2.3	13.0	
1965	0.6	9.1	
1966	0.1	−13.1	
1967	−1.4	20.1	Bull
1968	0.3	7.7	
1969	−1.2	−11.4	Bear
1970	3.6	0.1	
1971	1.9	10.8	
1972	1.3	15.6	
1973	3.1	−17.4	
1974	6.7	−29.7	
1975	7.2	31.5	
1976	4.3	19.1	
1977	0.8	−11.5	
1978	−0.3	1.1	Feb Low
1979	3.3	12.3	
1980	−2.2	25.8	Bull
1981	2.0	−9.7	
1982	−1.8	14.8	Bull

(Continued)

Table 9.1   (*Continued*)

New Year	Rally %	Year %	
1983	1.2	17.3	
1984	2.1	1.4	
1985	−0.6	26.3	Bull
1986	1.1	14.6	
1987	2.4	2.0	
1988	2.2	12.4	
1989	0.9	27.3	
1990	4.1	−6.6	
1991	−3.0	26.3	Gulf War
1992	5.7	4.5	
1993	−1.1	7.1	
1994	−0.1	−1.5	Flat
1995	0.2	34.1	
1996	1.8	20.3	
1997	0.1	31.0	
1998	4.0	26.7	
1999	1.3	19.5	
2000	−4.0	−10.1	Bear
2001	5.7	−13.0	
2002	1.8	−23.4	
2003	1.2	26.4	
2004	2.4	9.0	
2005	−1.8	3.0	Flat
2006	0.4	13.6	
2007	0.003	3.5	
2008	−2.5	−38.5	Bear
2009	7.4	23.5	
2010	1.4	12.8	
2011	1.1	−0.003	Flat

the S&P 500 had dropped 3 percent one week before the onslaught of the Persian Gulf War. This created a triple bottom at levels that will likely never be seen again.

Energy prices and Middle East terror woes may have grounded Santa in 2004. Early signs of recession and declining housing prices, which would eventually lead to financial crisis, spooked Santa in 2007. Previous absent Santa Claus Rallies in 1979 and 1981 preceded bear market lows in the following years of 1980 and 1982, respectively.

This indicator is most effective when confirmed by a down "First Five Days" and a down "January Barometer," covered in the next section.

January Jubilee

Namesake month of Janus, the Roman god of doorways and passages, January has quite a legendary reputation on Wall Street. Yale's January Barometer, of course, garners much of the notoriety with its .758 batting average since 1950. As the opening of the New Year, January is host to many important events, indicators, and recurring market patterns. U.S. presidents are inaugurated and deliver State of the Union addresses. New Congresses convene.

Financial analysts release annual forecasts. Residents of earth return to work and school en masse after holiday celebrations. Small stocks are rumored to outperform large stocks in the *nom de guerre*, the "January Effect." And, the largest number of my seasonal indicators occurs in January: day two marks the end of our Santa Claus Rally, the "First Five Days" is our first glimpse at the trading environment for the coming year and a whole month gain or loss of the S&P 500 triggers the January Barometer.

Ranked number one on NASDAQ (third on the Dow and the S&P 500) the last 41 years, January ends the year's best three-month span. NASDAQ has averaged a 2.8 percent gain since 1971. January's whole month performance is impressive but this dynamic month is also packed with important seasonality and telltale indicators. As the New Year commences cash flows from year-end bonuses and portfolio restructuring increase and flood the market. Analysts and market strategists try to decipher the market's tea leaves for the year ahead making January arguably the most important market month of the year.

Based on our market probability models January has a rather distinct trading pattern. The first trading day of the year normally keeps the New Year celebrations going—the Dow has been up 14 of the last 21 years and NASDAQ 13 of the last 21 years. However, the S&P 500 and Russell 2000 have been considerably weaker, with just nine and seven advances, respectively, over the same time frame.

It can be an opportune time to jump into the market, while traders are still groggy, ahead of a much stronger day two.

Over the next several days markets fluctuate with a slightly bearish bias. Then equities come alive around the 10th trading day of the month as the first mid-month 401(k) cash infusion is injected into the market. Buying also swells ahead of the first three-day weekend of the year, Martin Luther King Jr. Day. After this two- to three-day spurt stock prices sell off and meander until month-end. January expiration day has seen the Dow down 10 of the last 14 years, but it has been up 3 of the last 4. As January comes to a close stocks head higher with the last day of January being one of the stronger days of the year, especially for the Russell 2000.

January's First Five Days Early Warning System

Two early warning indicators surface the first several days of the month: the Santa Claus Rally and January's First Five Days. The seven-day Santa Claus Rally, which has averaged 1.5 percent for the S&P 500 since 1950, ends on the second trading day of January. This brief, reliable indicator is more significant in its absence. Times when this typical end-of-year bullishness has been missing have preceded bear markets or corrections.

January's First Five Days can provide a preliminary gauge of the year to come—especially when they are up.

Since 1950, 39 up First Five Days on the S&P 500 were followed by 33 full-year gains for an 84.6 percent accuracy ratio and a 13.6 percent average gain in those 39 years. The six exceptions include a flat 1994 and 2011 and four others related to war. Vietnam military spending delayed the start of the 1966 bear market. Ceasefire imminence early in 1973 raised stocks temporarily. Saddam Hussein turned 1990 into a bear. The war on terrorism, instability in the Middle East, and corporate malfeasance shaped 2002 into one of the worst years on record. Europe's sovereign debt crisis erased first half 2011 gains.

The 23 down First Five Days were not indicative—up 11, down 12. In post-election years, however, down First Five Days can be telling. Nine of the last 14 times the S&P 500 posted a loss for January's First Five Days; 6 of these 9 were followed by full-year losses averaging –11.1 percent. Five post-election First Five Days showed gains and four years followed suit, gaining 22.6 percent on average.

In midterm election years this indicator has had a spotty record—almost a contrary indicator. In the last 15 midterm years only 7 full years followed the direction of the First Five Days and only 1 has in the last 8. The full-month January Barometer (see next section) has a better midterm record of 66.7 percent accuracy.

Preelection years start with a stacked deck—the Dow has not been down since 1939. Only three First Five Days were down (1955, 1999, and 2007). All three posted full-year S&P 500 gains. Election years have followed the direction of the First Five Days 12 of the last 15 times though the S&P 500 has been down only three times in election years since 1950.

The Incredible January Barometer

Devised by Yale Hirsch in 1972, the January Barometer has registered only seven major errors since 1950 for an 88.7 percent accuracy rate. This indicator adheres to the maxim that as goes the S&P in January, so goes the year (see Figure 9.2). Of the seven major errors Vietnam affected 1966 and 1968; 1982 saw the start of a major bull market in August; two January rate cuts and 9/11 affected 2001; and the market in January 2003 was held down by the anticipation of military action in Iraq. The second worst bear market since 1900 ended in March of 2009 and Federal Reserve intervention influenced 2010. Including the eight flat years yields a .758 batting average.

Excluding 2001 and 2005, full years followed January's direction in the last 14 post-election years. Midterm years tracked January's direction 10 of the last 15. With the dice loaded for preelection years as mentioned previously, the January Barometer has a 15-and-1 record; the only

Figure 9.2   As Goes January, So Goes the Year: S&P 500 January Performance by Rank

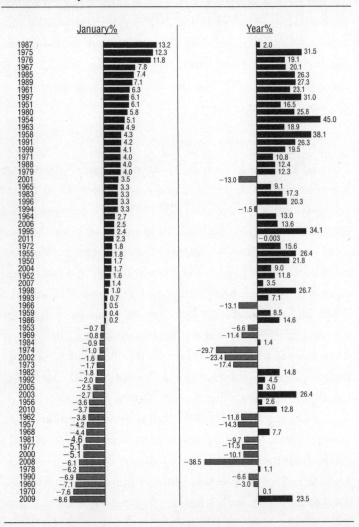

loss in 2003 due to exogenous events ahead of the military action in Iraq. Eleven of the last 15 election years have followed January's course.

Though some years posted full-year and 11-month gains, every down January since 1950 was followed by a new or continuing bear market, a 10-percent correction, or a flat year. Down Januarys have been followed by sub-stantial declines averaging –13.9 percent, providing excel-lent buying opportunities in most years.

Down Januarys are harbingers of trouble ahead, in the economic, political, or military arenas. Eisenhower's heart attack in 1955 cast doubt on whether he could run in 1956—a flat year. Two other election years with down Januarys were also flat (1984 and 1992). Thirteen bear markets began and nine continued into second years with poor Januarys. The year 1968 started down as we were mired in Vietnam, but Johnson's bombing halt changed the climate. Imminent military action in Iraq held January 2003 down before the market triple-bottomed in March. After Baghdad fell, preelection and recovery forces fueled 2003 into a banner year. The year 2005 was flat, registering the narrowest Dow trading range on record. January 2008 was the worst opening month on record and preceded the worst bear market since the Great Depression. A negative reading in 2010 preceded a 16-percent April to July correction, which was quickly reversed by the Fed's second round of quantitative easing or QE2.

Passage of the Twentieth "Lame Duck" Amendment to the Constitution in 1933 created the January Barometer. Since then it has essentially been "As January goes, so goes the year." January's direction has correctly forecasted the major trend for the market in most of the subsequent years.

Prior to 1934, newly elected senators and representatives did not take office until December of the following year, 13 months later (except when new presidents were inaugurated). Defeated congressmen stayed in Congress for all of the following session. They were known as "lame ducks." Since 1934, Congress convenes in the first week of January and includes those members newly elected the previous November. Inauguration Day was also moved up from March 4 to January 20.

January's prognostic power is attributed to the host of important events transpiring during the month: new Congresses convene; the president gives the State of the Union message, presents the annual budget, and sets national goals and priorities. These events clearly affect our economy and Wall Street and much of the world. Add to that, January's increased cash inflows, portfolio adjustments, and market strategizing and it becomes apparent how prophetic January can be. Switch these events to any other month and chances are the January Barometer would become a memory.

When the Dow closes below its December closing low in the first quarter, it is frequently an excellent warning sign. Jeffrey Saut, managing director of investment strategy at Raymond James, brought this to our attention a few years ago. The December Low Indicator was originated by Lucien Hooper, a *Forbes* columnist and Wall Street analyst back in the 1970s. Hooper dismissed the importance of January and January's first week as reliable indicators. He noted that the trend could be random or even manipulated during a holiday-shortened week. Instead, said Hooper, "Pay much more attention to the December low. If that low is violated during the first quarter of the New Year, watch out!"

Eighteen of the 32 occurrences were followed by gains for the rest of the year—and 16 full-year gains—after the low for the year was reached. All but two of the instances since 1952 experienced further declines, as the Dow fell an additional 10.9 percent on average when December's low was breached in Q1.

Only three significant drops occurred when December's low was not breached in Q1 (1974, 1981, and 1987). Both indicators were wrong only five times and nine years ended flat. In years that December's low is not crossed in Q1, the January Barometer is nearly 100 percent accurate.

Best Three Months

Be long November to January, historically the best consecutive three-month span to own stocks. Trading is generally holiday inspired with no significantly treacherous time frame. The Santa Claus Rally's official reading, given on the close of the second trading day of January, kicks off an indicator-packed January.

When Santa comes to town, the First Five Days, and January Barometer are all positive, which has occurred 27 times (includes 2012) in the last 63 years, full-year gains followed in 24 of the 26 previous occurrences, 92.3 percent of the time. Full-year S&P 500 gains have averaged 17.5 percent in these years.

At a Glance

- Be long November to January, historically the best consecutive three-month span to own stocks.
- As the S&P goes in January, so goes the year.

Chapter Ten

Spring Harvest

~

*Reaping the Produce of the
Best Six Months*

GROWING UP IN THE Northeast, February was always the
time when the big snowstorms hit and gave us a week off
from school for winter recess and getaways to Florida.
Those carefree days are long gone. I spend the early days
of February parading the airways and media outlets with
the results of the January Barometer and any adjustments
to my annual forecast. Then it's usually off to Traders
Expo New York that kicks off on President's Day.

Following solid gains in the best consecutive three-month span of November to January; markets usually take a breather in February. Depending upon the magnitude of January's gains, the market often corrects or consolidates in February. Any weakness can be used to add to existing long positions or to establish new ones as the market tends to resume its rally at the end of February or the beginning of March and continues to run until the end of the Best Six Months in April.

Once April does arrive, it is time to begin looking for early signs of seasonal weakness, tightening stop losses, and preparing for the Worst Six Months of the year. As volume begins to fade, market fundamentals and technical indicators are likely to confirm it is time to take profits on positions sown back in autumn weakness.

But let's start by looking at what good opportunities can be found in the first of the spring harvest months, February.

February Findings

January is a hard act to follow and the short, cold month of February is nearly forgotten on Wall Street and barely leaves a mark. Usually the weak link in the Best Six Months, February tends to follow the current trend, though big January gains often correct or consolidate during the month of valentines and presidents as Wall

Street evaluates and adjusts market outlooks based on January's performance. Since 1950, January S&P 500 gains of 2 percent or more corrected or consolidated in February 70.4 percent of the time. January losses were followed by February losses 62.5 percent of the time.

Since 1950, February is up only slightly more than half the time and, depending on the index, up or down marginally on average. However, small-cap stocks, benefiting from "January Effect" carryover, tend to outpace large-cap stocks in February. The Russell 2000 index of small-cap stocks has turned in an average gain of 1.0 percent in February since 1979—just the seventh best month for that benchmark.

Post-election year Februarys fare worse with the major indexes posting average losses. It is the worst NASDAQ month in post-election years averaging a –4.4 percent loss, down 8 of the last 10 times. Midterm and preelection year Februarys stand out from the month's overall performance, but rise only to mid-pack at best in these years. Election year Februarys, on the other hand, are a standout for NASDAQ and the Russell 2000. A very strong February in 2000 boosts NASDAQ and Russell 2000 rankings in election years. Otherwise, February's performance, compared to other presidential-election-year months, is mediocre at best with no large-cap index ranked better than ninth.

However, when both January and February were positive and the combined gain for the two months was at least 5 percent for the Dow, as was the case in 2012, this has been a bullish sign for the rest of the year. The previous 20 incidents since 1900 have led to gains from March to December 16 times for an average of 5 percent. The year 2011 was down a fraction, but nasty losses and bear markets occurred in 1930, 1931, and 1987.

After January's typically strong finish February opens well for large-cap stocks. The first trading day is bullish and it has traded higher in 15 of the past 21 years with an average S&P 500 gain of 0.5 percent. Strength fades after that until the stronger 8th, 9th and 11th trading days. Expiration week is marred by two bearish days and begins an often-weak second half of the month. Neither small caps nor technology shares completely escape mid-month weakness.

March Madness

Stormy March markets tend to drive prices up early in the month and batter stocks at month end. Named after Mars, the Roman god of war, the third month of the year often serves as a battleground for bulls and bears. Julius Caesar may not have heeded the famous warning to "beware the Ides of March," but investors would be served well if they did. Stock prices have a propensity to decline, sometimes rather precipitously, around mid-March. Remember, NASDAQ topped out on March 10, 2000, and the S&P peaked March 24, 2000. Most recent March gains have been logged in the beginning and middle of the month. The second half of the month is full of red ink and the last 3 or 4 days of the month have posted net declines in 16 of the last 22 years.

March packs a rather busy docket. It is the end of the first quarter, which brings with it Triple Witching and an abundance of portfolio maneuvers from the Street. March Triple-Witching Weeks have been quite bullish in recent years. But the week after is the exact opposite, with the Dow down 15 of the last 24 years—and frequently down sharply for an average drop of 0.5 percent. Notable Dow gains during the week after of 4.9 percent in 2000, 3.1 percent in 2007, 6.8 percent in 2009, and 3.1 percent in 2011 are the rare exceptions to this historically poor performing time frame.

Normally a decently performing market month, March is much weaker in post-election years with the Dow Jones Industrials and S&P 500 only eking out modest 0.2 percent and 0.4 percent gains, respectively. NASDAQ, on the other hand, slips to an average –0.7 percent loss. In midterm years performance is slightly above average. Preelection year Marches rank fourth and boast 2.0 percent average gains or better across the board. March is just average in election years with advances only 60 percent of the time and an average 0.5 percent Dow gain since 1952. S&P 500 has also advanced 60 percent of the time since 1952, but gains have been slightly better at 0.7 percent, on average. NASDAQ, however, has not fared well in March in election years since 1972. Due to a 17.1 percent loss in 1980, March is NASDAQ's worst month of the election year.

First days have been weaker for big-cap stocks, up about half the time. NASDAQ stocks and small-cap Russell 2000 stocks are slightly stronger in the beginning of March. By the sixth or seventh trading day things cool off until mid-month as the first Triple Witching of the year and 401(k) cash inflows tend to push stocks higher. After the Ides has past, market gains become scarce. Like the beginning of the month, small stocks and techs perform best the last day with the Russell 2000 up 76.2 percent of the time over the past 21 years while the Dow Jones Industrials are down 2 out every 3 years. This is reminiscent of the end of the second quarter when big caps lose ground and small stocks shine.

April Action

April was the first month to gain 1,000 DJIA points in 1999. However, from 2000 to 2005, tax month was hit hard, declining in four of six years. Since 2006, April has been up six years in a row with an average gain of 4.2 percent to reclaim its position as the best Dow month since 1950. April is second best for S&P 500 and Russell 2000 and third best for NASDAQ (since 1971).

April marks the end of our Best Six Months for the Dow Jones Industrials and the S&P 500. It also maintains a firm position in the other broad index Seasonal-Switching Strategies. When April comes around, especially if the market has recently rallied substantially, we began to look for our MACD (Moving Average Convergence Divergence) indicator seasonal sell signal for the Dow Jones Industrials and S&P 500.

The first half of April used to outperform the second half, but since 1994 that has no longer been the case. The effect of the April 15 tax deadline appears to be diminished. The market is clearly focused on first-quarter earnings during April. Exceptional Q1 earnings and positive surprises tend to be anticipated with stocks and the market moving up in advance of the announcements.

In post-election years April averages respectable gains with big moves up and down. Midterm Aprils are also peppered with wild swings but with a downside bias. Preelection Aprils are strongest for large-cap stocks with the S&P 500 down only once since 1950. Normally bullish election year influences (the second best year of the four-year presidential election cycle) have the exact opposite effect on April. Average gains since 1952 are approximately half of the average gain of all years since 1950 for the DJIA and S&P 500. Largely due to a 15.6 percent loss in 2000, NASDAQ's typical strength in all Aprils since 1971 is transformed into an average loss in election years.

Options expiration week frequently impacts the market positively in April and Dow stocks have the best track record since 1990, with an average gain of 1.6 percent for the week. The first trading day of expiration week has a slightly better record than expiration day, and the week as a whole is generally marked by respectable gains across the board. The week after, however, has often been ruled by sellers.

Even though April has been the top-performing Dow month over the past 62 years, it has experienced a fair share of volatility throughout the month. Sizeable one-day gains and losses have been quite commonplace recently. April's first several days are strongest for the Dow Jones Industrials and mid-month strength exists for stocks of all varieties. After the mid-month tax deadline the market has been prone to weakness, but the last three days of the month do exhibit more NADSAQ and Russell 2000 strength.

At a Glance

- February is usually the worst month of the Best Six Months, digesting the gains of the prior three months.
- Rallies typically resume through March and into April. But danger lurks as mid-month weakness in March and April tends to try the patience of traders and investors holding long positions with sizable profits.
- April is the best month of the year on average, but be on guard for signs of trouble. Taking profits and moving into defensive positions in April has proven prudent over the past 63 years.

Summer Doldrums

Why Summer Months Give Investors a Reason to Relax

IN RECENT YEARS, if you waited until May to sell and go away it was already too late. On May 6, 2010, traders and investors were blindsided by the first "flash crash." In a matter of minutes, the Dow plunged nearly 1,000 points but was able to recover much of the decline to close the day down only 347.80 points.

In 2011, May was the first of five consecutive declining months that would ultimately shave 16.8 percent off of the Dow from its April closing high to its October closing low. So spare yourself the pain and anguish of these months and consider exiting the market in April, and enjoy the start of warmer weather and a summer vacation.

May Matters

May has been a tricky month over the years. It used to be part of what we called the "May/June disaster area." From 1965 to 1984 the S&P 500 was down during May 15 out of 20 times. Then from 1985 through 1997, May was the best month, gaining ground every single year (13 straight gains) on the S&P, up 3.3 percent on average with the Dow Jones Industrials falling once and two NASDAQ losses.

In the years since 1997, May's performance has been erratic, up only 6 times in the past 15 years (4 of the years had gains in excess of 4 percent). NASDAQ suffered five May losses in a row from 1998 to 2001, down −11.9 percent in 2000, followed by six sizable gains in excess of 3 percent and three losses, the worst of which was 8.3 percent in 2010.

May begins the Worst Six Months for the Dow and S&P. To wit, "Sell in May and go away." Our Best Six

Months Switching Strategy, created in 1986, proves that there is merit to this old trader's tale. A hypothetical $10,000 investment in the Dow Jones Industrials compounded to $674,073 for November to April in 62 years compared to a $1,024 loss for May to October.

Post-election years, notoriously the worst years of the four-year election cycle, are May's best-performing year. In these years, May ranks number one on NASDAQ (average gain, 3.4 percent) and the Russell 2000 (average gain, 4.7 percent), second on the S&P 500 (average gain, 1.7 percent) and fourth on the Dow Jones Industrials (average gain, 1.3 percent).

Midterm election year Mays lose ground about half the time averaging losses across the board. Preelection year Mays are especially bullish for small stocks. The Russell 2000 averages a 2.7 percent advance in these rather bullish years.

Election year Mays rank at or near the bottom, registering net losses on the Dow Jones Industrials and NASDAQ, and fractional gains on the S&P 500 and Russell 2000.

The Monday before May option expiration is much stronger than expiration day itself albeit weaker for small caps. Big caps have only registered four losses in the last 22 years. Expiration day is a loser across the board. The full week had a bullish bias that has faded in recent years.

The week after options expiration week now favors tech and small caps. The Dow has fallen in 9 of the last 13 of these weeks.

On the Friday before Mother's Day the Dow Jones Industrials have gained ground 11 of the last 17 years but on the Monday after, the blue-chip average has risen in 14 of those years.

The first two days of May trade higher frequently, and the Dow Jones Industrials have been up four of the last five first trading days. NASDAQ and the Russell 2000 continue to be strong into day three and throughout the month. A bout of weakness often appears on the 3rd, 4th, 5th, 15th and 16th trading days for large-cap stocks, but the middle of the month tends to be rather strong. NASDAQ and the Russell 2000 take the lead again the last three days of May.

June Juju

The first month of summer has shone brighter on NASDAQ stocks over the last 41 years as a rule, ranking seventh with a 0.7 percent average gain, up 23 of 41 years. This contributes to NASDAQ's Best Eight Months, which ends in June. June ranks near the bottom on the Dow Jones Industrials just ahead of September since 1950.

NASDAQ's Best Eight Months have produced excellent long-term results. A hypothetical $10,000 invested in the NASDAQ composite only during the Best Eight Months (November to June), implementing a simple timing trigger since 1971, would have yielded a $1,011,221 gain versus a $7,305 loss during the Worst Four Months of July to October.

Post-election year Junes have been much weaker, pushing Dow and S&P average returns deeper into negative territory. Midterm election year Junes are the worst Dow, S&P 500, and Russell 1000 month. S&P 500 suffers the most, down 11 of 16 with an average loss of –2.1 percent. Preelection year Junes fare best, but have weakened recently with declines in 2007 and 2011.

The second Triple-Witching Week of the year brings on some volatile trading. On Monday of Triple-Witching Week the Dow has been up 12 of the last 22 years, but down 3 of the last 4. Triple-Witching Friday is slightly better, however, it is more prone to sizeable drops than gains. Full-week performance is choppy, littered with greater than 1 percent moves in both directions. Weeks after Triple-Witching Day are dangerous. This week has experienced Dow losses for 13 straight years, and there have been gains only twice in 22 years.

June's first trading day is the Dow's second best day of the month, up 15 of the last 21 years, only the 10th day is better with one additional advance. Gains are sparse throughout the remainder of the month until the last three days when semi-annual Russell index reshuffling pushes NASDAQ and Russell 2000 stocks highest. The last day of the second quarter is a bit of a paradox as "portfolio pumping" has driven the Dow down 15 of the last 21 years while buoying the NASDAQ and Russell 2000 higher in 13 and 14 of those years, respectively.

Every year when the days get long and the temperature rises on Wall Street, we always hear those infamous buzzwords, the "summer rally." As volume begins to shrink the hope for a summer rally catches the ear of investors. If such a rally does occur, it is often short-lived and unimpressive.

However, one notably exception does exist. NASDAQ has delivered a short, powerful rally that starts at the end of June on a consistent basis since 1987. This 12-day period from June's third to last trading day through July's ninth trading day has produced an average 2.3 percent gain over the years.

July Jolt

July may be the best month of the third quarter for the Dow and S&P, but that's not saying much. Performance for the other two months, August and September, is negative for the most part. Since 1950, the Dow has averaged a 1.2 percent gain while the S&P posts an average gain of 0.9 percent.

July begins NASDAQ's worst four months, and, except for a few select years, the over-the-counter index has been hit hard in July with an average gain of just 0.02 percent since 1971. Dynamic trading often accompanies the first full month of summer as the beginning of the second half of the year brings an inflow of new funds—likely from retirement accounts. This creates a bullish beginning, a weak middle, and strength toward the end (unless a bear market is in progress). Huge gains in July are often followed by sizeable drops and better buying opportunities later in the year.

Post-election Julys perform quite well and rank number one on the S&P 500 and the Dow Jones Industrials. Midterm election Julys are worst for the Russell 2000, ranking dead last. The Russell 2000 has been crushed over the years for a −4.3 percent drubbing and only two gains. Preelection Julys, swept up by overall bullish forces, achieve modest gains. Julys have suffered from the heat of the campaign trail in election years with large caps posting fractional gains and losses. Election year Julys are third worst on NASDAQ with an average drop of −1.8 percent, up four, down six.

Option expiration in July is generally characterized by flat trading. Monday before expiration has the strongest recent record, advancing in seven of the past nine years. Expiration Friday is moderately bearish with only 8 advances in the past 22 years. Expiration week and the week after have gone either way over the years with frequent weekly moves in excess of 2 percent.

The month opens strong with the Dow Jones Industrials and S&P 500 up 17 of the last 21 first trading days. Day two is weak followed by strength until options expiration. The third week of July, frequently the week after options expiration, is July's major trouble spot.

One of the many interesting seasonal patterns I have tracked over the years concerns July gains of 3.5 percent or more on the Dow that occurred since 1950. Table 11.1 illustrates that whenever bulls stampeded in July, investors were likely to be given an opportunity to purchase stocks cheaper sometime over the next few months.

Five times subsequent second half lows were reached rather quickly after hot July markets. The August 1954 low followed the bear market of 1953, when the market bottomed in September 1953 and went straight up until April 1956. August 1958's low followed the 1957 bear market, when the new bull market picked up steam in April 1958.

A quick low came in August 1970 as the 1969–1970 bear market ended in May 1970. The low arrived early in 2009 following the end of the second worst bear market

All other occasions brought better buying opportunities in the 90 days between mid-September and mid-December.

At a Glance

- "Sell in May and go away" is advice that exists for a good reason, but recent developing trends suggest this it may be dated. Selling in April the past two years was the prudent course of action.
- Aside from the 12-day NASDAQ summer rally, few opportunities will be missed by staying away from the market in June and July. Even when the Dow gains 3.5 percent or more in July, stocks have been cheaper to buy later in the year.

Chapter Twelve

Celebrate Good Times

~

Making the Most of Holiday Trading

EVERYONE NEEDS A BREAK now and then, even the markets and market-followers. The New York Stock Exchange (NYSE) closes nine times throughout the calendar year to celebrate select holidays, including New Year's Day, Martin Luther King Jr. Day, Presidents' Day, Good Friday, Memorial Day, Independence Day, Labor Day, Thanksgiving Day, and Christmas.

Obviously there are many other holidays and special occasions that people observe while the market remains open. But never fear. In the age of the smart phone, traders and investors can still access market data and make trades. Just don't let your mother catch you sneaking away to review and trade your investments. Although trading might be distracted during these times, most non-observed (by the NYSE) holidays have little discernable impact on the overall market. The exceptions are the Jewish High Holidays of Rosh Hashanah, Yom Kippur, and Passover—these exhibit influence on the markets, which we'll discuss later in the chapter.

Santa Claus Comes to Town

You might think we'd start by talking about the New Year holiday, but it's actually best to begin with the last holiday of the previous year, Christmas. Thanks to the Santa Claus Rally (the seven-trading-day period beginning after Christmas) the days before and after Christmas and New Year's Day are best for trading, especially tech stocks and small caps. NASDAQ and the Russell 2000 have averaged gains of 3.1 percent and 2.4 percent from three days before Christmas to three days after New Year's Day since 1990.

Gains can be contributed to year-end holiday spirit, year-end bonus payments, and the end of tax-loss selling. It doesn't hurt that these holidays fall in the Best Six Months of the year and right in the middle of the best consecutive three-month span.

Table 12.1   Trading Before and After Christmas Day Observances (since 1990)

	Day Before			Day After		
	# Advance	# Decline	Average %	# Advance	# Decline	Average %
DJIA	14	8	0.28	16	6	0.24
S&P 500	14	8	0.26	16	6	0.22
NASDAQ	14	8	0.51	17	5	0.25
Russell 2000	16	6	0.40	18	4	0.37

We regularly examine market action three days before and after a NYSE holiday, but the getaway day before and the day after are impacted most by the holiday. The market consistently revels the day before and after Christmas. Table 12.1 shows traders holiday shopping for stocks at Christmastime. I have gone back to 1990 for a better perspective of trading in recent years during both secular bull and bear markets.

Less bullishness on the last day is due to last-minute portfolio restructuring. Pushing gains and losses into the next tax year often affects the new year's first trading day. Recently this selling pressure has continued into the new year. This selling is evident by the negative average percent change for the Dow and S&P 500. And although the NASDAQ and Russell 2000 appear less negative, the NASDAQ has been down 10 of the last 11

Table 12.2   Trading Before and After New Year's Day Observances (since 1990)

	Day Before			Day After		
	# Advance	# Decline	Average %	# Advance	# Decline	Average %
DJIA	10	12	−0.23	15	7	0.40
S&P 500	8	14	−0.21	10	12	0.27
NASDAQ	12	10	0.04	14	8	0.22
Russell 2000	13	9	0.35	8	14	−0.14

last trading days of the year after rising for 29 straight years from 1971 to 1999. Russell 2000 has been down 9 of the last 11 years on the last day after 21 consecutive years of gains from 1979 to 1999. (See Table 12.2.)

Martin Luther King Jr. Day

Significant fourth-quarter rallies have a tendency to correct or consolidate in January. Over the years this trend has begun at different times in January. For example, in 2008 it started on day one, but in 2010, it began mid-month. Regardless of the actual starting point, mid-month January weakness has had a negative impact on the most recent holiday to be formally observed by the NYSE, Martin Luther King Jr. Day.

Recognition and observance of one of history's most important civil rights leaders on the third Monday of January every year since 1998 can delay the start of option's

Table 12.3 Trading around Martin Luther King Jr. Day Observance (since 1998)

	Day Before			Day After		
	# Advance	# Decline	Average %	# Advance	# Decline	Average %
DJIA	8	6	0.19	7	7	−0.33
S&P 500	9	5	0.25	7	7	−0.31
NASDAQ	9	5	0.26	7	7	−0.24
Russell 2000	10	4	0.23	7	7	−0.11

expiration week. A shortened trading week could also partly be responsible for the market's poor performance on Tuesday and frequently even worse trading action later in the week. Establishing a short position, into strength on the Friday before this three-day weekend, has the best odds of a profitable outcome in the following week. (See Table 12.3.)

Negative Presidents' Day

Presidents' Day is the lone holiday that exhibits weakness the day before and after. Trading has turned more negative over the last 22 years. The Friday before this midwinter three-day break is exceptionally bad, whereas the Tuesday after is not as brutal and has shown some improvement recently although average losses are greater for NASDAQ and the Russell 2000. (See Table 12.4.)

Table 12.4   Trading around Presidents' Day Observance (since 1990)

	Day Before			Day After		
	# Advance	# Decline	Average %	# Advance	# Decline	Average %
DJIA	6	16	−0.34	10	12	−0.33
S&P 500	5	17	−0.47	11	11	−0.44
NASDAQ	5	17	−0.68	6	16	−0.88
Russell 2000	10	12	−0.27	7	15	−0.64

Two unusually strong market showings in 1991 and 2003 were both related to military action in the Persian Gulf. In 1991 the month-long punishing air war waged by coalition forces to liberate Kuwait from Saddam Hussein's August 1990 invasion began to impact Iraqi forces. On February 15, 1991, the Friday before Presidents' Day, Iraq's offer to pull out of Kuwait for the first time tied to lifting sanctions was rejected by President Bush as a "cruel hoax." The following Tuesday after the holiday, General Schwarzkopf said Iraqi forces were "on the verge of collapse." These two clear signs of capitulation were celebrated on Wall Street with buying. In February 2003 the Dow had dropped 13.2 percent from the previous November high as the anticipation of another fray into Iraq loomed over the world. As the invasion of Iraq became imminent the market rallied the day before and after Presidents' Day before falling to its final 2003 low the week before the March 19 offensive.

Leading up to the Friday before Presidents' Day the market is quite strong three days before the holiday weekend. You can use this strength to lock in profits before you leave for the slopes or the islands. If you plan to stick around and trade, consider setting up a short trade to capitalize on market weakness that often plagues this time of year. Friday has the most consistent record of declines, but those losses do not frequently carry over into Tuesday, making Friday the best day to cover any short positions. Hopefully you will enjoy presidential profits around this brief mid-winter holiday.

The Luck of the Irish

Saint Patrick's Day is the only recurring holiday in March. Sure, Good Friday and Easter land in March from time to time, but it's only happened 12 times in the past 62 years. Saint Patrick's Day, however, occurs on the same day every year. Although there is no official stock market closing or bank holiday it is celebrated by millions (perhaps billions) of people every year. And the festivities do hit close to Wall Street. Parades are held worldwide, but the largest runs right up the center of Manhattan. New York City has hosted an annual parade since 1762.

Gains on Saint Patrick's Day or the day after when it falls on the weekend have been greater and much more consistent than the day before. Anticipation of the patron

Table 12.5   Trading around St. Patrick's Day (since 1990)

	Day Before			March 17 or the Day After*		
	# Advance	# Decline	Average %	# Advance	# Decline	Average %
DJIA	12	10	0.22	16	6	0.62
S&P 500	14	8	0.18	17	5	0.66
NASDAQ	11	11	−0.11	15	7	0.71
Russell 2000	9	13	−0.19	16	6	0.61

*Either March 17 or the following trading day when St. Patrick's Day falls on a weekend.

saint's holiday and preparations for the parade down Fifth Avenue may cause equity markets to languish. Perhaps the absence of those participating in the festivities drives the snakes out of Wall Street, leaving only the strongest professional hands to gather up the gold at the end of the rainbow. Or maybe it's the fact that Saint Pat's usually falls in Triple-Witching Week. Table 12.5 illustrates that since 1990 the market is weaker before Saint Patrick's Day, but only suffered a handful of losses the day of or after.

A "Better" Good Friday

Good Friday is the one NYSE holiday with a clear positive bias before and negativity the day after. NASDAQ is up 15 of the last 17 days before Good Friday and 11 straight since 2001. The day after Easter has the second

Table 12.6   Trading around Good Friday Observance (since 1990)

	Day Before			Day After		
	# Advance	# Decline	Average %	# Advance	# Decline	Average %
DJIA	15	7	0.48	11	11	−0.08
S&P 500	15	7	0.53	9	13	−0.13
NASDAQ	16	6	0.58	11	11	−0.29
Russell 2000	16	6	0.61	6	16	−0.21

worst post-holiday record; losses are steeper after Presidents' Day. The S&P 500 was down 16 of 20 years on the day after Easter, but it has been up 6 of the last 8 years. Table 12.6 shows a strong market before Good Friday and weakness after.

When Good Friday falls in April, the day before is more positive than when it lands in March. The S&P 500 is up 9 of the last 11 times the holiday fell in April. The day after Easter is still negative when the holiday falls in April, though less so than when it occurs in March. This is likely related to March's end-of-quarter volatility and the overall bullishness of April, the best Dow month of the year.

Memorial Day and the Stock Market

Congress voted to recognize Memorial Day at the end May with the National Holiday Act of 1971. Since

Table 12.7   Trading around Memorial Day Observance (since 1990)

	Day Before			Day After		
	# Advance	# Decline	Average %	# Advance	# Decline	Average %
DJIA	11	11	−0.17	15	7	0.27
S&P 500	11	11	−0.10	11	11	0.20
NASDAQ	11	11	−0.08	12	10	0.32
Russell 2000	12	10	−0.01	11	11	0.29

1971, Memorial Day has been observed on the last Monday in May. Memorial Day has had a weak bias ahead of the long weekend and strength after the holiday. Early departures for the first long summer weekend have driven the Dow down in three of the last four years.

The week after Memorial Day has been sporadic, following the short-term trend of the market. The Dow Jones Industrials was up 12 years in a row from 1984 to 1995. The last 16 years it has been up 7 times with some substantial, triple-digit gains in 1999, 2000, 2003, and 2007 to 2009. However, in the past two years there have been substantial declines: 204.66 in 2010 and 290.32 in 2011 (see Table 12.7).

Few Fireworks on Independence Day

Trading on the day before and after the Independence Day holiday is often lackluster. Volume tends to decline on either side of the holiday as vacations begin early and since 1900 in March. The now-famous Jackson Hole, Wyoming, speech where Fed Chairman Ben Bernanke first spoke of a QE2 quickly put a floor under the market in 2010.

Table 11.1 Hot July Markets and Autumn Buying Opportunities

July Gains of 3.5% or More			Subsequent Second Half Low		
Year	Dow	% Gain	Date	Dow	% Lower
1951	257.86	6.3	Nov 24	255.95	−0.7
1954	347.92	4.3	Aug 31	335.80	−3.5
1956	517.81	5.1	Nov 28	466.10	−10.0
1958	502.99	5.2	Aug 18	502.67	−0.1
1959	674.88	4.9	Sep 22	616.45	−8.7
1962	597.93	6.5	Oct 23	558.06	−6.7
1967	904.24	5.1	Nov 08	849.57	−6.0
1970	734.12	7.4	Aug 13	707.35	−3.6
1973	926.40	3.9	Dec 05	788.31	−14.9
1978	862.27	5.3	Nov 14	785.26	−8.9
1980	935.32	7.8	Dec 11	908.45	−2.9
1987	2572.07	6.3	Oct 19	1738.74	−32.4
1989	2660.66	9.0	Oct 13	2569.26	−3.4
1991	3024.82	4.1	Dec 10	2863.82	−5.3
1994	3764.50	3.8	Nov 23	3674.63	−2.4
1997	8222.61	7.2	Oct 27	7161.15	−12.9
2005	10640.91	3.6	Oct 21	10215.22	−4.0
2009	9171.61	8.6	Aug 17	9135.34	−0.4
2010	10465.94	7.1	Aug 26	9985.81	−4.6
			Total		−131.4
			Average		−6.9

Table 12.8 Trading around Independence Day Observance (since 1990)

	Day Before			Day After		
	# Advance	# Decline	Average %	# Advance	# Decline	Average %
DJIA	12	10	0.03	9	13	0.03
S&P 500	12	10	0.03	11	11	−0.07
NASDAQ	11	11	−0.06	9	13	−0.09
Russell 2000	11	11	−0.18	9	13	−0.16

finish late. Although improving modestly in recent years, since 1980, DJIA, S&P 500, NASDAQ, and Russell 2000 have recorded average losses on the day before and the day after. The same summertime vacation theme consisting of early departures and late returns is the most likely culprit. (See Table 12.8.)

Trading the Labor Day Markets

For many people, Labor Day weekend is the prime vacation time. Back in the first half of the twentieth century approximately one-fourth of the country worked on farms as compared with less than 2 percent nowadays. Business activity ahead of the long weekend was more energetic in the old days. From 1950 through 1977 the three days before Labor Day pushed the Dow Jones Industrials higher in 25 of 28 years. Since then bullishness has shifted to the last day before and the two days after. This frequently

Table 12.9   Trading around Labor Day Observance (since 1990)

	Day Before			Day After		
	# Advance	# Decline	Average %	# Advance	# Decline	Average %
DJIA	11	11	0.09	13	9	0.26
S&P 500	11	11	0.09	12	10	0.25
NASDAQ	12	10	0.15	12	10	0.16
Russell 2000	15	7	0.10	10	12	0.22

coincides with early September strength. While positive across-the-board gains on the day before and after are prevalent since 1990, the frequency of these gains is only slightly better than half the time. The small caps of the Russell 2000 have the most consistent record of gains on the day before. (See Table 12.9.)

Sell Rosh Hashanah, Buy Yom Kippur, Sell Passover

There is an old saying on Wall Street, "Buy Rosh Hashanah, Sell Yom Kippur." Though it had a good record at one time, it stopped working in the middle of the last century. Still, it gets tossed around every autumn when the High Holidays are on the minds of traders as many Jewish colleagues take off to observe the Jewish New Year and Day of Atonement. But we have observed that the wiser course of action has been to Sell Rosh

Hashanah, Buy Yom Kippur, Sell Passover. The basis for the new pattern is that with many traders and investors busy with religious observance and family, positions are closed out and volume fades creating a buying vacuum. (See Table 12.10 for the details.)

When the holiday falls on a weekend the prior market close is used. It's no coincidence that Rosh Hashanah and Yom Kippur fall in September or October, two dangerous and opportune months. Passover conveniently occurs in March or April, right near the end of our Best Six Months Switching Strategy.

Perhaps it's Talmudic wisdom but selling stocks before the eight-day span of the High Holidays has avoided many declines, especially during uncertain times like 2008. Being long Yom Kippur to Passover has produced more than twice as many advances, averaging gains of 6.7 percent. This trade worked particularly well in 2009, 2010 and 2011. It often pays to be a contrarian when old bromides are tossed around, buying instead of selling Yom Kippur.

Trading the Thanksgiving Market

For 35 years the combination of the Wednesday before Thanksgiving and the Friday after had a great track record, except for two occasions. Attributing this phenomenon to the warm holiday spirit was a no-brainer. But publishing it in the *1987 Stock Trader's Almanac* was the

Table 12.10   Sell Rosh Hashanah, Buy Yom Kippur, Sell Passover

	Rosh Hashanah to Yom Kippur Dow % Change	Yom Kippur to Passover Dow % Change
1971	−2.7	6.4
1972	−1.7	0.9
1973	2.3	−12.7
1974	−0.3	20.7
1975	−3.9	22.1
1976	−3.1	−5.2
1977	−1.8	−3.2
1978	4.1	−3.4
1979	−2.3	−10.1
1980	2.7	4.3
1981	4.2	−4.0
1982	0.4	22.8
1983	−1.5	−5.0
1984	−2.4	6.5
1985	0.3	39.6
1986	1.4	25.3
1987	2.1	−24.7
1988	1.0	13.7
1989	3.7	−2.2
1990	−4.1	18.8
1991	0.2	11.6
1992	−3.0	7.1
1993	−2.5	6.5
1994	1.8	6.4
1995	−0.5	19.9
1996	1.0	15.9
1997	0.4	11.8
1998	0.7	25.4
1999	−1.9	0.2
2000	−0.8	−7.4
2001	−2.7	19.8
2002	−0.6	−0.5

Table 12.10   (*Continued*)

	Rosh Hashanah to Yom Kippur Dow % Change	Yom Kippur to Passover Dow % Change
2003	3.0	10.2
2004	−1.8	1.1
2005	−3.0	9.0
2006	1.4	7.2
2007	2.9	−7.0
2008	−20.9	−5.8
2009	−0.3	11.4
2010	1.8	15.6
2011	−0.5	17.6
Average	−0.7	7.0
# Up	18	28
# Down	23	13

kiss of death. Wednesday, Friday, and Monday were all crushed, down 6.6 percent over the three days in 1987. Since 1988 Wednesday to Friday gained 14 of 24 times with a total Dow point gain of 451.20 versus Monday's total Dow point loss of 619.07, down 9 of 13 since 1998.

Roles were reversed in 2011. Wednesday and Friday got slammed 263 Dow points and bounced 291 points the following Monday. European debt concerns, signs of slowing growth in China, and another budget deal failure in Washington, D.C., caused the worst Thanksgiving week since 1932 and the third worst loss since 1901. But a 16.4 percent increase in holiday shopping over the weekend and news that European leaders were advancing

Table 12.11   Trading around Thanksgiving Day Observance (since 1990)

	Day Before			Day After		
	# Advance	# Decline	Average %	# Advance	# Decline	Average %
DJIA	14	8	0.17	13	9	0.13
S&P 500	14	8	0.22 ·	13	9	0.17
NASDAQ	16	6	0.39	16	6	0.49
Russell 2000	15	7	0.36	17	5	0.30

a plan to deal with the region's debt crisis resulted in market advances across the board on Monday.

Dubai's debt crisis cancelled Black Friday on Wall Street in 2009; DJIA shed 154.48 in the day's shortened trading session. All four indexes have declined on the day after Thanksgiving the past three years. The best strategy seems to be going long into weakness Tuesday or Wednesday and staying in through the following Monday or exiting into strength prior. (See Table 12.11.)

At a Glance

- Thanks to the Santa Claus Rally, the days before and after Christmas and New Year's Day are best. However, trading around the first day of the year has been mixed. Traders recently have been selling more the first trading day of the new year.

- Bullishness before Labor Day and after Memorial Day is affected by strength the first day of September and June. The second worst day after a holiday is the day after Easter. Surprisingly, the following day is one of the best second days after a holiday, right up there with the second day after New Year's Day.
- Presidents' Day is the least bullish of all the holidays—bearish the day before and three days after. NASDAQ has dropped 17 of the last 22 days before Presidents' Day (Dow, 16 of 22; S&P, 17 of 22; Russell 2000, 12 of 22).
- Like the other recurring stock market cycles there is an ebb and flow surrounding holiday trading. The patterns are never exactly 100 percent the same. Exogenous events knock them off kilter, and they change gradually over time with the shifts in human behavior and social traditions.

Chapter Thirteen

Don't Sell on Friday

Human Behavior Still Shapes Market Activity

THROUGHOUT THE HISTORY of the *Stock Trader's Almanac* the stock market's performance has been examined on a yearly, monthly, weekly, daily, and on a half-hourly basis to uncover its trends and tendencies. Over the course of nearly a half-century's worth of research it has been proven time and time again that the beginning, ending, and middle of months, weeks, and days have significance.

This should not come as a shock to members of the human race. We place a great deal of emphasis on the start and finish of nearly everything in our lives. From our simple daily, everyday routines and throughout our entire time alive we encounter and cope with the beginning and end of events. Sometimes the start is encountered with anxiety, sadness, and fear while on other occasions it is merrily celebrated. Endings are the same.

Such importance does, in fact, carry over into the stock market. After all, it is people that are trading and investing everyday that the market is open. Yes, computers are heavily involved now, but it was humans who programmed them to do what they do.

Most Gains Occur on Monday and Tuesday

Since 1990, Monday and Tuesday have been the most consistently bullish days of the week for the Dow and Thursday and Friday the most bearish, as traders have become reluctant to stay long going into the weekend. Mondays and Tuesdays gained 11,992.54 Dow points, while Thursday and Friday combined for a total loss of 2,677.45 points. In past flat and bear market years, Friday was the worst day of the week and Monday the second worst. In bull years, Monday is best and Friday number two. In Table 13.1 when the market is closed on a Monday holiday Tuesday's results are used. When the market is closed for a Friday holiday, Thursday data are used.

Monday, Most Favored S&P 500 Day

Between 1952 and 1989 Monday was the worst trading day of the week. In Figure 13.1 the first trading day of

Table 13.1 Annual Dow Point Changes for Days of the Week Since 1990

Year	Monday*	Tuesday	Wednesday	Thursday	Friday*	Dow Close	Year's Change
1990	219.90	−25.22	47.96	−352.55	−9.63	2633.66	−119.54
1991	191.13	47.97	174.53	254.79	−133.25	3168.83	535.17
1992	237.80	−49.67	3.12	108.74	−167.71	3301.11	132.28
1993	322.82	−37.03	243.87	4.97	−81.65	3754.09	452.98
1994	206.41	−95.33	29.98	−168.87	108.16	3834.44	80.35
1995	262.97	210.06	357.02	140.07	312.56	5117.12	1282.68
1996	626.41	155.55	−34.24	268.52	314.91	6448.27	1331.15
1997	1136.04	1989.17	−590.17	−949.80	−125.26	7908.25	1459.98
1998	649.10	679.95	591.63	−1579.43	931.93	9181.43	1273.18
1999	980.49	−1587.23	826.68	735.94	1359.81	11497.12	2315.69
2000	2265.45	306.47	−1978.34	238.21	−1542.06	10786.85	−710.27
2001	−389.33	336.86	−396.53	976.41	−1292.76	10021.50	−765.35
2002	−1404.94	−823.76	1443.69	−428.12	−466.74	8341.63	−1679.87
2003	978.87	482.11	−425.46	566.22	510.55	10453.92	2112.29
2004	201.12	523.28	358.76	−409.72	−344.35	10783.01	329.09
2005	316.23	−305.62	27.67	−128.75	24.96	10717.50	−65.51
2006	95.74	573.98	1283.87	193.34	−401.28	12463.15	1745.65
2007	278.23	−157.93	1316.74	−766.63	131.26	13264.82	801.67
2008	−1387.20	1704.51	−3073.72	−940.88	−791.14	8776.39	−4488.43
2009	−45.22	161.76	617.56	932.68	−15.12	10428.05	1651.66
2010	1236.88	−421.80	1019.66	−76.73	−608.55	11577.51	1149.46
2011	−571.02	1423.66	−776.05	246.27	317.19	12217.56	640.05
2012**	514.63	−21.71	75.52	304.79	121.25	13212.04	994.48
Totals	6522.51	5070.03	1143.75	−830.53	−1846.92		10458.84

*Monday denotes first trading day of week, Friday denotes last trading day of week.
**Partial year through March 30, 2012.

[189]

Figure 13.1   S&P 500 % Performance Each Day of the Week, June 1952 to December 1989

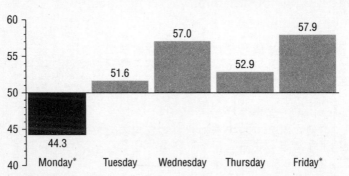

Based on the number of times S&P 500 closed higher than previous day.
* Monday denotes first trading day of week; Friday denotes last trading day of week.

the week (including Tuesday when Monday is a holiday) rose only 44.3 percent of the time, while the other trading days closed higher an average of 54.8 percent of the time. (NYSE Saturday trading discontinued June 1952.)

As you can see in Figure 13.2 a dramatic reversal occurred in 1990—Monday became the most powerful day of the week. However, during the last 11.33 years Tuesday has produced the most gains. Since the top in 2000, traders have not been inclined to stay long over the weekend nor buy up equities at the outset of the week. This is not uncommon during uncertain market times. Monday was the worst day during the 2007 to 2009 bear and only Tuesday was a net gainer. Since the March 2009 bottom, Monday is best.

Bear Hurts Monday and Friday

To determine if market trend alters performance of different days of the week, we compared 22 bear market years to 38 bull market years. While Tuesday and Thursday did not vary much between bull and bear years, Mondays and Fridays were sharply affected. There was a swing of 10.5 and 9.5 percentage points in Monday's and Friday's performance, respectively. (See Table 13.2.)

NASDAQ Strong Like Bull

Despite 20 years less data, daily trading patterns on NASDAQ through 1989 in Figure 13.3 appear

Figure 13.2   S&P 500 % Performance Each Day of the Week, January 1990 to March 30, 2012

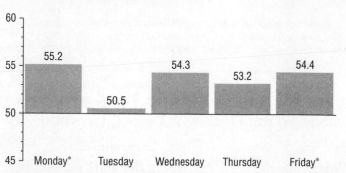

Based on the number of times S&P 500 closed higher than previous day.
Monday denotes first trading day of week; Friday denotes last trading day of week.

Table 13.2   S&P 500 % Performance Each Day of the Week June 1952–2011

	Monday	Tuesday	Wednesday	Thursday	Friday
All 61 Years	47.9 %	51.4 %	56.0 %	52.6 %	56.5 %
38 Bull Years	51.8 %	52.8 %	58.5 %	53.4 %	60.0 %
22 Bear Years	41.2 %	48.9 %	51.8 %	51.3 %	50.5 %

Most Wednesdays closed last seven months of 1968.
Monday denotes first trading day of week, Friday denotes last trading day of week.

Figure 13.3   NASDAQ % Performance Each Day of the Week, 1971–1989

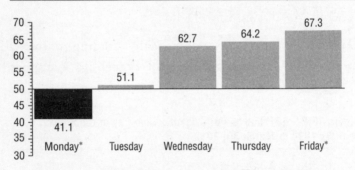

Based on the number of times NASDAQ closed higher than previous day prior to February 5, 1971, from National Quotation Bureau indexes.
* Monday denotes first trading day of week; Friday denotes last trading day of week.

to be fairly similar to the S&P 500 except for more bullishness on Thursdays. During the mostly flat markets of the 1970s and early 1980s, it would appear that apprehensive investors decided to throw in the towel over weekends and sell on Mondays and Tuesdays.

Figure 13.4   NASDAQ % Performance Each Day of the Week, 1990 to March 30, 2012

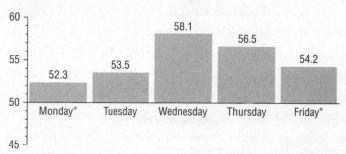

Based on the number of times NASDAQ closed higher than previous day prior to February 5, 1971, from National Quotation Bureau indexes.
*Monday denotes first trading day of week, Friday denotes last trading day of week.

Notice the vast difference in Figure 13.4 in the daily trading pattern between NASDAQ and S&P from January 1, 1990, to recent times. The reason for so much more bullishness is that NASDAQ moved up 1,010 percent, over three times as much during the 1990–2000 period. The gain for the S&P was 332 percent and for the Dow Jones Industrials, 326 percent.

After dropping a hefty 77.9 percent from its 2000 high (versus –37.8 percent on the Dow and –49.1 percent on the S&P 500), NASDAQ tech stocks still outpace the blue chips and big caps but not by nearly as much as they did. From January 1, 1971, through May 4, 2012, NASDAQ moved up an impressive 3,199 percent. The Dow (up 1,454 percent) and the S&P (up 1,386 percent) gained just over less than half as much.

Monday's performance on NASDAQ was lackluster during the three-year bear market of 2000 to 2002. As NASDAQ rebounded (up 50 percent in 2003) strength returned to Monday during 2003–2006. During the bear market from late 2007 to early 2009, weakness was most consistent on Monday and Friday. NASDAQ's weekly patterns are beginning to move in step with the rest of the market.

Traders Take Lunch, Too

Half-hourly data became available for the Dow Jones Industrial Average starting in January 1987. Examination of half-hourly performance from 1987 to 2012 in Figure 13.5

Figure 13.5   Dow % Performance Each Half-Hour of the Day, 1987 to April 2012

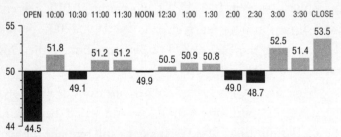

Based on the number of times the Dow Jones industrial average increased over the previous half-hour.

shows early morning and mid-afternoon weakness with end-of-day strength.

It is usually the weak hands, or individuals, who try to sell first thing in the morning after having reevaluated their positions overnight or over the weekend. Brokerage houses oblige buying their clients shares on the cheap pushing prices higher before lunch.

Traders eat, too, and you can see prices flatten out as Wall Street participants take a moment to sustain themselves from noon to 2 P.M. Around this time the pros get positioned for the big move at the end of the day and stocks tend to fall from two to three. The end of the day is when institutions and professional traders firm up positions driving prices higher the last hour on most days.

I separated half-hourly trading since January 1987 by day of the week to see how the typical week behaves. After an opening sell-off on Monday the market snaps back in the second half hour and then is quite flat until 3 P.M. Monday closes are the strongest followed closely by Friday's close.

Mid-week mornings are generally down with Thursday the worst. Friday tends to open stronger and drift flat to down until the last hour of the day. On all days stocks tend to firm up near the close with weakness early morning and from 2 P.M. to 2:30 P.M. frequently. Weakness near the close, especially on Friday and Monday can be indicative of a precarious market ripe for a fall.

At a Glance

- Fear, joy, and greed are facts of life. Trading has become increasing electronic, but human nature remains an integral influence.
- Weakness at the beginning and end of the day and/or week is a sign that confidence is waning. Strength begets strength.
- Daily habits and patterns have left an indelible mark on intraday market action.

Chapter Fourteen

Picking the Ripe Trade

~

When the Season Is Right, Indicators Are Strong, and Timing Is Perfect

THE INVESTING HIGHWAY is littered with the abandoned vehicles of traders who never made it—they either failed to stick to a sensible methodology or never had one to begin with.

Some traders take a hands-off approach to investing by hiring a professional money manager while others actively manage their own funds. You need to find out what makes the markets tick so that you can make better trading and investing decisions whatever your style may be. The strategies discussed in this chapter show how clear and simple it is to recognize that a cycle or pattern is setting up well for a trade, that conditions are ripe, and how to recognize when a technical indicator has given a signal to buy or sell. But first, let's take a look at just how far we've come over the past several decades.

A Chance for the Individual Trader

Back in the old days it was much more difficult to implement trading strategies based on patterns and cycles. The process was limited to large institutions, well-heeled investors, and sophisticated traders. They were the only ones with the capital resources or know-how to set up and fund the complex derivative trading strategies or unit investment trusts required to capitalize on these trends.

But with the advent of exchange traded funds (ETFs), the individual investor or trader has more tools at his fingertips to trade practically any index, sector, commodity, bond, or other asset class. Take for example the widely followed blue-chip stock index, the Standard & Poor's 500. The S&P 500 is an index of the 500 biggest and most influential stocks in the world.

Before 1993 the only way to trade the S&P 500 was through expensive futures contracts, risky index options, or some form of unit trust or wrap fee agreement that a brokerage firm would bundle up and sell shares to high-net-worth individuals. Then the ETF was invented. The first ETF was issued on the S&P 500. It packaged all 500 stocks in a new security.

This ETF is informally known as the Spyder. The nickname is taken from the name (SPDR S&P 500) and trading symbol (SPY). SPDR stands for Standard & Poor's Depository Receipts. It is unit trust that the public can trade freely on the stock exchange. Each share represents the value of one-tenth of the S&P 500 index. Instead of paying $1,400 for one share of the S&P you can buy one share of SPY for $140.

Investing and trading strategies have many different time horizons depending on the trader. While I am not a day trader by any stretch of the imagination I do believe there is a time to buy and hold and a time to be a more active trader. As the saying goes, "A rising tide lifts all ships." So before we get into shorter-term portfolio maneuvers it is important to have a clear understanding of the big picture—where the market is in respect to the longer term cycles. This will guide how aggressive or conservative you should be overall.

WHAT ARE EXCHANGE-TRADED PRODUCTS?

ETPs are a security based on another investment. They can be benchmarked to indexes, commodities, currencies, baskets of stocks, bonds, and so forth, or they can be actively managed funds. ETPs are priced and trade intraday on a major securities exchange. Exchange-traded products include exchange-traded funds (ETFs), exchange-traded vehicles (ETVs), exchange-traded notes (ETNs), and certificates.

ETFs are the most widely used and prolific ETP. They actually hold assets that track stock indexes, commodities, currencies, or other baskets of assets, but they trade just like a stock. ETFs provide the diversification of an index fund with the ability to trade intraday, sell short, buy on margin, and trade options. In addition, expense ratios are significantly lower than those of mutual funds.

Exchange traded notes are a bit different. ETNs also trade intraday on a major exchange like a stock, but they are an unsecured, unsubordinated, debt security. The credit rating of the issuer may impact the value of an ETN. ETNs combine aspects of bonds and ETFs. Investors may hold the ETN until maturity like a bond when they can receive cash equal to the principal amount on the day of maturity. ETNs can be quite effective if issued by a reliable firm, especially for trading commodities and volatility indexes (like the VIX).

ETVs are open-ended, collateralized, secured, debt securities created and redeemed on demand by multiple market makers.

For Everything There Is a Season

Back in the 1970s when the Vietnam War had become unbearable, Nixon had taken the United States off the gold standard and OPEC had levied its oil embargo against us, my father was the first to call the bottom of the last secular bear market. At the tender age of eight I will never forget his October 1974 newsletter headline: "BUY! BUY! BUY!" 18 times across the top.

As the years went by I learned the entire business from the ground up. Every year since December 2001, when I made my first annual forecast, I have been analyzing and forecasting market moves with—thankfully—a good deal of success. These forecasts and the constant reevaluating during the year of where the market is with respect to these cycles are what guide our trading. Once we establish where we are in any or all of the cycles at any given time we employ fundamental and technical trading tactics to confirm buy and sell decisions.

Our lists of seasonal trades (see Table 14.1 and Table 14.2) have been refined immensely over the past decade as weak ones have been weeded out and new ones have emerged. It's important to be sure the holdings, methodology, or strategy of the trading vehicle you choose closely matches the underlying market or sector you wish to trade or invest in.

Table 14.1 Top Stock Sector Index Seasonality Trades

Ticker	Sector Index	Type	Start	Seasonality	Finish	
XCI	Computer Tech	Short	January	B	March	B
IIX	Internet	Short	January	B	February	E
XNG	Natural Gas	Long	February	E	June	B
RXP	Healthcare Prod	Long	March	M	June	M
RXH	Healthcare Prov	Long	March	M	June	M
MSH	High-Tech	Long	March	M	July	B
XCI	Computer Tech	Long	April	M	July	M
IIX	Internet	Long	April	M	July	B
CYC	Cyclical	Short	May	M	October	E
XAU	Gold & Silver	Short	May	M	June	E
S5MATR*	Materials	Short	May	M	October	M
BKX	Banking	Short	June	B	July	B
XNG	Natural Gas	Short	June	M	July	E
XAU	Gold & Silver	Long	July	E	December	E
DJT	Transports	Short	July	M	October	M
UTY	Utilities	Long	July	E	January	B
BTK	Biotech	Long	August	B	March	B
RXP	Healthcare Prod	Long	August	B	February	B
MSH	High-Tech	Long	August	M	January	M

IIX	Internet	Long	August	B	January	B
SOX	Semiconductor	Short	August	M	October	E
CMR	Consumer	Long	September	E	June	B
RXH	Healthcare Prov	Short	September	M	November	B
XOI	Oil	Short	September	B	November	E
BKX	Banking	Long	October	B	May	B
XBD	Broker/Dealer	Long	October	B	April	M
XCI	Computer Tech	Long	October	B	January	B
CYC	Cyclical	Long	October	B	May	M
RXH	Healthcare Prov	Long	October	E	January	M
S5MATR*	Materials	Long	October	M	May	M
DRG	Pharmaceutical	Long	October	M	January	B
RMZ	Real Estate	Long	October	E	May	B
SOX	Semiconductor	Long	October	E	December	B
XTC	Telecom	Long	October	M	December	E
DJT	Transports	Long	October	B	May	B
XOI	Oil	Long	December	M	July	B

B = Beginning Third, M = Middle Third, and E = Last Third of the month.

*S5MATR available @ bloomberg.com

Source: Stock Trader's Almanac.

Table 14.2   Top Commodity Seasonality Trades

Commodity	Contract	Years	Trading Day	Hold Days
January				
S&P 500 Peaks (Short)	H	1983–2011	2	12
Euro Peaks (Short)	H	1999–2011	3	24
Wheat Peaks (Short)	N	1970–2011	3	85
S&P 500 Bottoms (Long)	H	1983–2011	15	7
February				
30-Year Bond Peaks (Short)	M	1978–2011	3	44
Yen Bottoms (Long)	M	1977–2011	6	62
Soybeans Bottoms (Long)	N	1969–2011	9	73
Crude Oil Bottoms (Long)	N	1984–2011	10	60
Gold Peaks (Short)	J	1975–2011	13	17
Silver Peaks (Short)	K	1973–2011	13	45
Sugar Peaks (Short)	N	1973–2011	14	39
Natural Gas Bottoms (Long)	N	1991–2011	16	41
March				
Cocoa Peaks (Short)	N	1973–2011	10	23
Yen Peaks (Short)	M	1977–2011	10	14
Euro Peaks (Short)	M	1999–2011	11	9
British Pound Bottoms (Long)	M	1976–2011	15	22
April				
30-Year Bond Bottoms (Long)	U	1978–2010	18	81
S&P 500 Bottoms (Long)	U	1982–2010	18	28
May				
Cattle Peaks (Short)	V	1976–2010	2	30
Copper Peaks (Short)	N	1973–2011	8	13
Silver Peaks (Short)	N	1973–2010	10	29
Coffee Peaks (Short)	U	1974–2010	16	54
British Pound Peaks (Short)	U	1975–2010	20	8

Table 14.2 (*Continued*)

Commodity	Contract	Years	Trading Day	Hold Days
June				
30-Year Bond Bottoms (Long)	U	1978–2010	2	10
Cocoa Bottoms (Long)	U	1973–2010	2	24
Soybeans Peak (Short)	U	1970–2010	5	36
Wheat Bottoms (Long)	Z	1970–2010	6	105
Sugar Bottoms (Long)	V	1975–2010	11	32
Cattle Bottoms (Long)	J	1970–2010	14	160
Corn Peaks (Short)	U	1970–2010	18	25
British Pound Bottoms (Long)	U	1975–2010	20	16
July				
S&P 500 Peaks (Short)	U	1982–2010	10	7
Natural Gas Bottoms (Long)	X	1990–2010	17	62
Cocoa Peaks (Short)	Z	1973–2010	18	70
August				
Swiss Franc Bottoms (Long)	Z	1975–2010	6	48
Coffee Bottoms (Long)	Z	1974–2010	12	13
Cocoa Bottoms (Long)	Z	1973–2010	14	24
Gold Bottoms (Long)	Z	1975–2010	18	25
September				
Euro Bottoms (Long)	Z	1999–2010	5	16
Crude Oil Peaks (Short)	G	1983–2010	8	62
Cocoa Peaks (Short)	Z	1973–2010	10	33
British Pound Bottoms (Long)	Z	1975–2010	12	33
October				
Silver Peaks (Short)	Z	1972–2010	4	17
Yen Peaks (Short)	H	1976–2010	12	78
Soybeans Bottoms (Long)	F	1968–2010	16	12
Euro Bottoms (Long)	H	1999–2010	18	47

(*Continued*)

Table 14.2   (Continued)

Commodity	Contract	Years	Trading Day	Hold Days
S&P 500 Bottoms (Long)	H	1982–2010	19	41
Corn Bottoms (Long)	N	1968–2010	20	133
November				
Lean Hogs Bottoms (Long)	G	1969–2010	2	13
Cocoa Bottoms (Long)	H	1972–2010	4	34
Gold Bottoms (Long)	G	1975–2010	13	10
30-Year Bond Peaks (Short)	M	1977–2010	14	107
Swiss Franc Bottoms (Long)	H	1975–2010	18	24
December				
Wheat Bottoms (Long)	K	1970–2010	5	20
Corn Bottoms (Long)	N	1970–2010	6	22
Copper Bottoms (Long)	K	1972–2010	10	47
British Pound Peaks (Short)	M	1975–2010	19	56
Swiss Franc Peaks (Short)	H	1975–2010	19	41

Source: Commodity Trader's Almanac.

Seasonality works well when range-bound markets bounce and during long booms as I expect will materialize in 2017 or 2018. When the secular bear market is officially declared over sometime in the next several years, back up the truck and load up on stocks. Whether you are positioning your portfolio for the long haul or making tactical maneuvers to increase capital gains and income, the following trading strategies will without a doubt increase your performance.

When I first put together my 15-year projection (now 13 years in Figure 4.1) for the Dow in March 2011 to accompany my super boom forecast for Dow 38,820 by 2025, I took into consideration the long-term cycles discussed in this *Little Book* in conjunction with current events and conditions. Market action at the time, what we knew of geopolitical plans, fundamentals, and global economic conditions were also factored into my calculus. Over the past year or so, things have played out relatively close to my projections. The Dow did not touch or pierce 10,000 in 2011, but it came quite close—about 10,400 intraday on October 4, 2011.

I take a similar tack for the annual forecast. Near-term economic data, seasonal pattern performance, and market conditions have a greater impact, though I still consider where we are in the long-term cycles. I don't make these annual and long-term forecasts just for the press and the sake of it. These forecasts and projections are the basis and framework for my trading activity. However, I am not married to these outlooks and am not reticent about changing my stance if conditions warrant.

This was the case in 2008, for example. Seasonal patterns were entirely off kilter in late 2007 and early 2008. After Bear Stearns went down I pulled the plug and went into cash. I declared a recession and bear market were under way in March 2008. Then I started getting bullish in November when the Dow hit 7,500. Don't ever underestimate the power of factoring stock market cycle analysis into your investment and trading decisions.

It's All about the Timing

So how do you combine cycles, fundamentals, and timing to increase profits and cut losses short. First and foremost, October is the best month of the year to buy stocks. Secondly, the most statistically sound, simple stock market trading strategy I know is my Best Six Months Switching Strategy.

Most people who know something about the stock market have heard the phrase "Sell in May and go away." It comes from an old British saw, "Sell in May and go away, come back on St. Leger day." Established in 1776, the St. Leger Stakes is the last flat thoroughbred horse race of the year and the final leg of the English Triple Crown. Apparently once the British horse-racing season concludes everyone can get back to the business of buying stocks.

While the St. Leger Stakes has little to do with stock market seasonality, it does coincide with the end of the worst months of the year for stocks. We have proven over the years that most of the markets gains occur in the six-month period from November to April. If you don't buy in October or November what do you have to sell in May or better yet April? My Best Months Switching Strategy will not make you an instant millionaire as other strategies claim they can do. What it will do is steadily build wealth over time with half the risk (or less) of a buy-and-hold approach. (Take a look back at Chapter 6 for a detailed discussion of the Best Six Months Switching Strategy . . . it works!)

Use of the words buy and sell often creates some confusion. They are often interpreted literally, but this is not necessarily the situation. Exactly what action an individual investor or trader takes when we issue our official fall buy or spring sell recommendation depends upon that individual's goals and risk tolerance.

A more conservative way to execute our switching strategy, or "the in-or-out approach," entails simply switching capital between stocks and cash or bonds. During the Best Months an investor or trader is fully invested in stocks. Index tracking ETFs and mutual funds are an easy and inexpensive way to gain stock exposure. During the Worst Months capital would be taken out of stocks and could be left in cash or used to purchase a bond ETF or bond mutual fund.

This approach works very well for retirement accounts where the goal is steady, consistent gains with limited risk. Of further benefit, you will probably find summertime vacations and activities much more enjoyable because you will not be concerned with stock market gyrations while your nest egg is parked in the safety of cash or bonds. Since 1950, there have only been nine years when the DJIA failed to deliver market gains during the Best Six Months.

Another approach involves making adjustments to your portfolio in a more calculated manner. During the Best Months additional risk can be taken as market gains are expected, but during the Worst Months risk needs to be reduced, but not entirely eliminated. There have been several strong Worst Months periods over the past decade such as 2003 and 2009. Taking this approach is similar to the in-or-out approach, however, instead of exiting all stock positions a defensive posture is taken.

Weak or underperforming positions can be closed out, stop losses can be raised, new buying can be limited, and a hedging plan can be implemented. Purchasing out-of-the-money index puts, adding bond market exposure, and/or taking a position in a bear market fund would miti-gate portfolio losses in the event a mild summer pullback manifests into something more severe such as a full-blown bear market.

Generally speaking, during the Best Months you want to be invested in equities that offer similar exposure to the companies that constitute Dow, S&P 500, and NASDAQ indexes. These would typically be large-cap growth and value stocks as well as technology concerns. Reviewing the holdings of a particular ETF or mutual fund and comparing them to the index members is an excellent way to correlate. During the Worst Months switch into Treasury bonds, money market funds, or a bear/short fund.

Taking a Good, Hard Look at the Indicators

The key here is using a technical indicator in conjunction with other tools like our Best Six Months strategy to confirm or assist in timing buy and sell decisions. So once we enter April or October we begin tracking our indicators for a buy or sell signal.

MACD, the Moving Average Convergence/Divergence indicator, developed and popularized by Gerald Appel, provides a uniquely sensitive measurement of the intensity of the trading public's sentiment and provides early clues to trend continuation or reversal. According to Appel, this indicator is particularly dependable in signaling entry points after a sharp decline. The MACD indicator may be applied to the stock market as a whole or to individual stocks or mutual funds.

The MACD indicator uses three exponential moving averages: a short or fast average, a long or slow average, and an exponential average of the difference between the short and long moving averages, which is used as a signal line. (See moving averages below for a discussion on simple and exponential moving averages.)

- MACD reveals overbought and oversold conditions for securities and market indexes and generates signals that predict trend reversals with significant accuracy.

- MACD produces less frequent whipsaws, as compared with moving averages.

- A type of shorthand refers to MACD indicators. An "8-17-9 MACD," for example, uses a short (fast) moving average of 8 days or weeks, a long (slow) moving average of 17 days or weeks, and an exponential moving average of 9 days or weeks. (The use of days or weeks depends on the time span of the stock graph. It could also be months or minutes or any duration depending on the frequency of each data point.)

- Gerald Appel recommends an 8-17-9 MACD to generate buy signals and a 12-25-9 MACD to confirm a sell signal for a stock, which has had a strong bullish move.

- Regardless of the accuracy of this indicator, one should not rely on a single indicator. Study as many technical and fundamental indicators as possible before arriving at your investment decisions.

So what's an exponential moving average?

A simple moving average is calculated by totaling the closing prices of a stock over a prescribed period (say, 30 days) and dividing that total by the number of days in the period (i.e., 30). The resulting number is the average. In order for the average to move, the most recent closing price is added to the previous total and the oldest closing price used in that total is subtracted. The new total is then divided by the number of days of the moving average, and the process repeated.

Changes in the upward or downward trend of the stock being measured are identified by the stock price or index crossing over its moving average, as well as a change in direction of the moving average itself. According to the moving average theory, when a stock price moves below its moving average, a change is signaled from a rising to a declining market; when a stock price moves above its moving average, the end of the declining trend is signaled.

A disadvantage of the simple moving average approach is that it will allow an extreme high or extreme low to distort the true value of the stock, possibly giving false buy or sell signals or rapid whipsaws.

To overcome the distortion caused by extreme highs or lows, the exponential moving average weights recent closing prices more heavily than earlier closing prices. Many market technicians consider the exponential moving average to be a more accurate indicator than a simple moving average.

What's a signal?

- A buy signal (positive breakout) is given when the MACD graph is in an oversold condition below the origin and the MACD line crosses above the signal line.

- A sell signal (negative breakout) is given when the MACD graph is in an overbought condition above the origin and the MACD line falls below the signal line.

- Significant MACD signals occur far from the zero line. When the MACD line is far from the zero line, it shows that the public is reacting to the emotion of the trend. Thus, when the crowd surges in the opposite direction and a crossover occurs, the implication is strong. Crossovers in the vicinity of the zero line suggest that public emotion is flat and disinterested and often do not lead to productive moves.

- The amount of divergence between the MACD line and the signal line is important—the greater divergence, the stronger the signal.

MACD is just one of many technical indicators that will help you make better buy and sell decisions. The trick is finding one or more that makes sense to you. Once you have some success stick with it. You can always add in more indicators or switch to different ones that give clearer signals at different times.

Have Sound Trading Discipline

So remember, first you must establish that the market or security is tracking the relevant pattern closely and setting up well for the trade. Common sense tells you whether or not the trade is fundamentally sound with respect to current market conditions and valuations. Then the trade is executed using one or more simple technical indicators.

These same trading techniques can be used for all your investment decisions. They can be applied to individual stocks you like for noncyclical reasons, or to select a stock within a favored sector. It also works for general market timing. I hope you enjoy making sound investments decisions and successful trades as you build your assets and protect your portfolio!

Acknowledgments

———— ∾ ————

To Christopher Mistal, my director of research and business partner, I can't thank you enough for your help in completing this project.

I would also like to thank all the folks at John Wiley & Sons, especially Kevin Commins, Pamela van Giessen, and Joan O'Neil for their unrelenting support; Meg Freeborn for her astute and tireless efforts editing and helping me polish the manuscript; and Robin Factor and Stacey Fischkelta for diligently seeing this project through to production.